Learning Begins

Learning Begins

The Science of Working Memory and Attention for the Classroom Teacher

Andrew C. Watson

ROWMAN & LITTLEFIELD
Lanham • Boulder • New York • London

Published by Rowman & Littlefield
A wholly owned subsidiary of The Rowman & Littlefield Publishing Group, Inc.
4501 Forbes Boulevard, Suite 200, Lanham, Maryland 20706
www.rowman.com

Unit A, Whitacre Mews, 26-34 Stannary Street, London SE11 4AB

British Library Cataloguing in Publication Information Available

Library of Congress Cataloging-in-Publication Data Available

ISBN 978-1-4758-3336-2 (cloth : alk. paper)
ISBN 978-1-4758-3337-9 (pbk. : alk. paper)
ISBN 978-1-4758-3338-6 (electronic)

♾™ The paper used in this publication meets the minimum requirements of American
National Standard for Information Sciences—Permanence of Paper for Printed Library
Materials, ANSI/NISO Z39.48-1992.

Printed in the United States of America

To H3
Who makes everything better, including this book.

Contents

About A Teacher's Guide to the Learning Brain Series

In the twenty-first century, teachers have increasingly turned to brain scientists—psychologists and neuroscientists—to understand how students learn. This emerging field of Mind Brain Education weaves together the practical know-how of classroom teachers and the scientific knowledge of scholars.

A Teacher's Guide to the Learning Brain series brings together the most important conclusions of this transdisciplinary work, exploring its best-researched and most useful conclusions. By explaining psychology and neuroscience with clarity and humor, and by illuminating their research conclusions with real-world classroom examples, this series helps teachers make learning easier and teaching more effective.

The first book, *Learning Begins*, considers the science of **working memory** and of **attention**. In this volume, teachers learn how students integrate new knowledge and new skills with their current memory systems. By exploring the surprising complexity of human attention systems, teachers also learn how to help students focus on essential learning goals.

The second book, *Learning Deepens*, explores more affective and physical processes: **emotion, motivation, and the body**. By understanding the connection between feeling and learning, teachers move beyond a purely cognitive approach to learning in order to shape their students' full learning environment.

The final book, *Learning Thrives*, studies the formation of **long-term memories**—both in the brain (as new neural networks) and in the mind (as new learning). Teachers who understand the specific processes that encode, consolidate, and retrieve new memories can help students change their brains and change their minds.

Taken together, *A Teacher's Guide to the Learning Brain* series makes Mind Brain Education clear, exciting, and useful for classroom teachers.

Preface

My first two years of teaching—like yours, perhaps—were chaotic, baffling, and joyous: full of impossible challenges and rich in unlikely, tiny victories. Despite all my worries, my department chair gave me enthusiastic evaluations, my colleagues reassured me during times of angst, and my students laughed at my jokes.

Given all these promising signs, I thought, I just might have what it takes to be a teacher.

During my third year, the English department at my school developed a writing test for all our Sophomores to take. We wanted to have a consistent benchmark to ensure that our students learned essential skills: how to hone a thesis, how to sculpt crisp sentences, how to quote with panache.

Being a third-year veteran—a grizzled pro, in my own mind—I was confident that my students would hit that test out of the park. You can imagine my emotions when so many swung and missed.

After a day of stunned moping, I scheduled a meeting with Jane, my department chair. She listened to my sad report, then said this:

"Andrew, all the best teachers I know want to be better teachers."

In part, Jane's words offered me present comfort. Although I was, at that moment, woefully aware of the progress I needed to make, Jane saw that discomfort as the mark of a good teacher, not a bad one.

More importantly, in the long run, Jane helped me recognize an essential quality for good teaching: the desire to be better at teaching.

Almost certainly, that's why you're reading this book. You're a good teacher, and you want to be a better one.

The good news: lots (and LOTS) of people have advice about being a better teacher.

The bad news: teachers might struggle to sort through all the possibilities. So many new approaches seem plausible that it's hard to know which one to select. Should I flip my classroom? Should I emphasize projects? Will a one-to-one laptop program help my students learn? Can team teaching, or the Harkness method, or instructional rounds, or group work, or a focus on introversion make my classroom better?

And, what should I do when these ideas conflict with one another?

For my first two decades as a teacher, I stayed focused on my colleagues and my discipline. With so many wise and experienced teachers in my department, and so many authors to study in the field of English, I had much to glean about teaching, learning, and literary creativity.

And then, almost ten years ago, I started to think about the part of the body that does the teaching, the learning, and the creating: the *brain*. Since it's my job to help students change their brains, shouldn't I know more about that grey matter I've heard so much about?

Over these last ten years—first as an independent explorer, then as a neuroscience/psychology graduate student, and now as a professional development consultant—I've learned three truths:

- First, brain science is *fascinating*—especially for teachers. (Very few teachers say to me: "Brains? Huh. I don't care.") People love learning about this baffling and powerful part of our body.
- Second, brain science is *complicated*. I used to think that adolescent behavior is counterintuitive, jargon-laden, technology-dependent, and argumentative. But trust me when I tell you: brain-science-world is even more counterintuitive, jargon-laden, technology-dependent, and argumentative. Teachers can easily get lost in this seductive galaxy of complexities.
- Third, brain science is *useful*. Once we start to master some of the complexity, we find useful new perspectives, and classroom-ready teaching strategies.

This series of books helps teachers understand complex brain research in psychology and neuroscience. As we wrestle with this material, we can both *think differently* about our classrooms, and *do things differently* in the classroom.

My goal, in other words, is to make current brain research clear *and* practically useful for teachers, schools, and classrooms.

Learning Begins includes insights, guidelines, and suggestions—but few rules. Here's why: *people are different*. A veteran sixth-grade social studies teacher at a small suburban school has one set of questions, needs, quirks, and skills. Of course, a novice second-grade teacher at a large inner-city parochial school has a different set. Likewise, a mid-career high-school Latin teacher at an exam school differs from those two, and—probably—from you.

Your students are different. Your schools are different. Your curricula are different. And—crucially—*you* are different. Teachers can't switch from role to role as if we were Lego bricks. So too, a specific teaching strategy that works well in one context might well be counterproductive in another.

For this reason, *Learning Begins* offers new ways to think about learning, and describes teaching strategies that align with them. However, the final decision—"given my personality, what specific strategy works best with my students and my curriculum in my school"—must rest with individual classroom teachers.

To emphasize this point, *Learning Begins* frequently encourages you to stop reading and write down connections between the research under discussion and your particular classroom. Every reader will—and should—process these ideas differently; the more time you spend drawing specific links between brain science and your own practice, the more helpful the book will be.

Just as teachers differ from one another, so too our students. In all of the cognitive capacities discussed in this book—especially *working memory* and *attention*—teachers can expect quite a broad range of behavior and capacity among our students. That variety is normal; again, people are different. When teachers know more about the science of working memory and attention, we can be more effective in our work across this broad range.

In fact, I hope to persuade you that teachers should *not* study brain science only to learn about diagnosable problems: students, for example, with diagnosed working memory deficits, or with ADHD. For too many years, a research-informed perspective has been focused on too few students.

Instead, schools and teachers should recognize that—given the busy complexity of the school day—*all of our students* face difficulties with working memory and attention. The scientific approach that helps us work with diagnosable students can be just as helpful with all our students. This wider group is, in fact, the focus of this book.

(Teachers who work with diagnosed students should rely on in-school experts and licensed professionals. This book's guidance will doubtless help teachers understand their suggestions, but it should not substitute for them.)

Learning Begins focuses on scientific research that offers practical guidance to teachers. Because the nitty-gritty of research methodology is, at times, so important to understanding particular conclusions and strategies, I have described several studies in detail. At the same time, I have tried to keep those descriptions clear and lively; for this reason, I occasionally simplify some of the more complex research procedures. The studies themselves—all of which are cited in the text—offer full descriptions of research methodology.

My focus on brain research raises an important philosophical point. I do not argue—and do not believe—that teachers should simply read up on psychology and neuroscience and then do what the researchers tell us to do.

Even if we wanted to do that, we can't. Researchers work by isolating variables; schools work by combining variables. No single study, no pool of studies, can ever answer the complex questions that teachers need answered every day.

Instead, I believe that psychologists *and* neuroscientists *and* teachers have valuable and helpful ways of thinking about learning. The goal of this book is to weave these strands of thought together into a stronger rope. A conversation among our disciplines will help all three, and—most important of all—help our students learn.

Learning Begins introduces you, and welcomes you, to that conversation.

Introduction

Part I of *Learning Begins* introduces the science of *working memory*.

As chapter 1 demonstrates, working memory allows students to combine multiple pieces of information together into some novel form: a new word, a new sentence, a new dance move, and a new idea. In other words, most kinds of academic learning are simply impossible without effective working memory functioning. Because working memory is both crucial and alarmingly small, teachers have to be skillful at working within its vexing limitations.

Chapter 2 starts developing this skill by exploring two burning questions: How can teachers *anticipate* working memory problems before they occur? And, how can we *recognize* them when they do occur? Happily, both research and experience offer teachers practical guidance to answer these questions.

Chapter 3 turns to every teacher's favorite question: how can we *solve these problems*? That is, once we learn to anticipate and identify working memory overload (in chapter 2), what research-aligned strategies can lighten that load? We explore both explicitly cognitive strategies, and strategies that focus more on students' emotional processes.

To conclude Part I, chapter 4 briskly reviews chapters 1–3, and then applies their suggestions to a specific lesson plan. By reviewing and correcting a syllabus that introduces the topic of "trophic cascade," we get concrete practice anticipating, identifying, and solving working memory problems. Chapter 4 also answers several Frequently Asked Questions: the questions I hear most often when I work with teachers interested in working memory.

Like Part I, Part II introduces a topic from cognitive science and then devotes several chapters to practical classroom solutions.

Chapter 5 begins with a surprising scientific conclusion about that most precious of classroom commodities: *attention*. From a psychological and neuroscientific perspective, attention is not one unified process: not, in other words, one thing that students can pay. Instead, attention results from three other mental processes, which researchers call *alertness, orienting*, and *executive attention*. Teachers can help students conjure attention not by focusing on attention itself, but instead by concentrating on those three subprocesses.

Chapters 6–8 then look at each of these processes in turn. In chapter 6, we consider classroom strategies that moderate students' alertness levels. We have lots of research—and lots of experience—to help keep students in the optimal alertness zone.

Chapter 7 explores the complex subject of orienting. To help students orient appropriately, we first need to identify and reduce the disorienting stimuli in the classroom environment. This process requires teacherly focus on everything from radiators to iPads. We also need to rethink our efforts to make classroom work engaging, unifying, and meaningful.

Chapter 8 considers the most abstract of the three attentional subprocesses: executive attention. In particular, it discusses the most puzzling of inattentional symptoms: *students seeming to think about a question the wrong way*. (That is, not simply getting the wrong answer.) This discussion, in turn, leads to several well-researched solutions.

Chapter 9 summarizes the material on attention. It then practices the strategies under discussion by reviewing a lesson plan on the Peninsular Campaign during the American Civil War. The FAQs at the end of chapter 9 help sort through the nuances and implications of attention research.

Any series of books that brings together psychology, neuroscience, and pedagogy has a lot of ground to cover. For the sake of convenience, *A Teacher's Guide to the Learning Brain* divides research into distinct topics.

This book, *Learning Begins*, focuses primarily on working memory and attention. The second book in this series focuses on more affective components of the learning process: emotion, motivation, self-control, and the body. The third book, in turn, looks at specific processes that build long-term memories—both in the brain (as new neural networks) and in the mind (as new learning).

By dividing the science of learning into these subcategories, *A Teacher's Guide to the Learning Brain* makes this material easier to understand, and its lessons easier to apply. At the same time, these divisions are—of course—artificial. All of these mental processes influence each other in powerful and important ways.

For instance, as will be discussed in chapter 8, problems with *executive attention* might be solved by reducing *working memory* load. As seen in chapter 3, *working memory* problems might be exacerbated by *emotional* overload, such a stress. And, of course, teachers care about *attention* and *emotion* and *working memory* primarily because they help explain *long-term memory* formation.

The more that teachers learn about specific topics in psychology and neuroscience, the more we understand how they influence each other, and our students' learning.

In *The Neuroscience of Human Relationships* (2006), Louis Cozolino argues that there is no such thing as a single human brain. He means that all of our brains were, quite literally, developed by interacting with dozens, hundreds, even thousands of other people. Absent those interactions with other brains, my individual brain would not exist.

Over these last several months, I've learned a related truth: there is no such thing as a single human author.

I mean that, quite literally, this book grew out of my interactions with dozens of authors, scholars, and professors, hundreds of colleagues, and thousands of students. Absent those connections, this book would not exist.

The people listed below have been especially helpful in creating this book: reading and correcting many drafts; offering wisdom, counsel, and support; and inspiring me to teach and to learn in the first place. Any factual inaccuracies or stylistic quirks are, of course, my own responsibility. But the strengths of *Learning Begins* draw substantially on the contributions of these people, to whom I am truly grateful:

Jane Archibald, Alice Baxter, Maya Bialik, Joanna Christodoulou, Betsy Conger, Patty Cousins, Lisa Damour, David Daniel, Rachel Engelke, Kurt Fischer, Mary Forrester, Phyllis Grinspan, Tina Grotzer, Paul Harris, Heath Hightower, Sarah Jubar, Gigi Luk, Mara Lytle, Scott MacClintic, Kevin Mattingly, Jonathan Mulrooney, Todd Rose, Stephanie Fine Sasse, Jeff Scanlon, Lawrence Smith, Lynette Sumpter, Judy Watson, Glenn Whitman, and Michael Wirtz.

Andrew Watson
Somerville, MA
September, 2016

Part I

WORKING MEMORY

Chapter One

Memory at Work

Imagine this scenario:

A lifelong friend has a big birthday coming up, and so you decide to go all out on a gift. Your friend loves photographs, and so you commit to creating an epic photo album—one that tells a decades-long story of camaraderie.

You dig through all your storage—photo albums, manila folders, old shoe boxes—and pick the liveliest photos you can find. Of course, hundreds don't make the cut, but you're looking for the one-of-a-kind photos that capture the zest of your friendship.

You spread the photos out on a table and contemplate their order. You start with a chronological presentation, but a year-by-year album feels predictable and generic. You re-sort the photos by event: all the backpack vacations, all the New Year's parties, all the look-at-us-now selfies. Still dissatisfied, you keep sliding the photos around on the table, searching for just the right layout.

Believe it or not, this photo album quest very much resembles your students' most common cognitive work.

How can this be? Let's consider an example.

In your American History class, you ask students to contemplate this question: How did the French and Indian War set the stage for the American Revolution?

To develop an answer, your students first rummage through their mental archives. They know lots of information about those wars (just as you have lots of photographs with your friend). But only a small percentage of that information is useful in answering the question, and so your students leave most of that knowledge on their mental shelves (just as you left most of the photos in your shoe boxes).

Once students have selected the most important ideas, they hold them in an active cognitive workspace (much like your sorting table). They then rearrange all those facts, trying several different structures until one stands out as the best (much as the perfect photo album emerges after all that reshuffling). Voila: an answer! (Epic photo album!)

In both cases, the quality of the final product depends on three variables. First, just as you need good photos among all the mediocre ones, so too your students need the right ideas and facts in their *long-term memory* banks. Second, just as you temporarily relocate those photos to a table, your students need to hold a few relevant facts in *short-term memory.* And third, just as you rearrange photos, they need to *reshuffle ideas into different mental layouts*— looking for the most persuasive order.

All analogies are imperfect, and this one certainly has its flaws. But if teachers think about cognitive activity as a photo-album construction project, we immediately see several important truths.

First, memory is much more complicated than we thought.

Because we have the single word *memory*, we are tempted to believe that memory is one cognitive process. Presumably the brain has a memory area— the part of the brain that does the remembering.

And yet, during more than hundred years of research, psychologists and neuroscientists have mapped the extraordinary complexity of our memory processes (Kandel, 2006; Milner, Squire, & Kandel, 1998; Squire, 2004). Depending on whose nomenclature we use, we have eight or ten or twelve different memory systems. They function distinctly from each other and often take place in different neural networks across multiple brain regions. For example, *declarative memory* stores information that is true or false, and can be stated out loud. If your lifelong friend asks you to name the capital of North Dakota, you are in for some well-deserved mockery if you say "Pierre." (The correct answer, as any German chancellor knows, is "Bismarck." "Pierre" is the capital of South Dakota—just ask any French prime minister.)

Procedural memory, on the other hand, stores knowledge of how to do something. Muscle memory, for example, is a kind of procedural memory. Years ago, when your friend asked for help in learning to ride a bike, you probably spent more time demonstrating than explaining. After all, riding a bike requires more how-to (procedural) knowledge than factual (declarative) knowledge.

When your students look through their long-term memory stores to answer your history question, they rely on both declarative and procedural memory. For instance, they *know that* George Washington accompanied General Braddock on an ill-fated expedition to Fort Duquesne—a kind of factual knowledge. They also *know how* to think about your question. They should, for example, interrogate their sources of information.

A second truth that this analogy highlights is that you can't make a good photo album without a big-enough table top to sort through all the images, and your students can't ponder questions without enough cognitive working space to sort through all the facts.

Imagine, for example, you tried to rearrange all of your photos on the fold-up end table next to your couch. That end table is just too small, and you would almost immediately run out of room. Photos would tumble off the edges. You would spend so much time crawling on the floor reaching under your couch that you couldn't possibly think clearly about your photo album plan.

Likewise, your students might quickly run out of cognitive workroom. They know that Washington learned about military order and strategy from Braddock's expedition; they know that he used this knowledge to command Revolutionary forces. They know that the French and Indian War cost the British government shocking sums; they know that Parliament raised Colonial taxes to make up those losses. Yet relatively quickly, as they recall all these specific bits of knowledge, their mental workspace fills up. By the time they have gathered enough data from declarative memory to answer the question, they may well have run out of room on their mental table.

This analogy, however imperfect, forces teachers to reexamine our priorities. Of course, we want to ensure our students form specific long-term memories: facts, procedures, skills, character traits, and habit of mind. We want them to get those photographs into albums. Yet to do so, our students need to do lots of rearranging. To make that rearranging possible, we need to focus zealously on end tables.

END TABLE ESSENTIALS

Psychologists have a name for that end table: they call it *working memory.* We use our working memory any time we both hold information in short-term memory and then rearrange or combine that information into some new cognitive structure (Baddeley, 2003).

For teachers to understand the role of working memory (WM) in learning, we must recognize three essential characteristics: its uses, its limitations, and its development.

Working Memory at Work and Play

As noted above, working memory allows us to hold information and to reorganize it into a new mental structure: a new word, a new sentence, a new concept, a new map, and a new argument. As you consider that definition, you'll see that we use WM all the time.

If you and your friend try to remember all the states you have visited together, you are pulling information from your long-term memory into your short-term memory (Cowan, 2008). If you then decide to put those states in alphabetical order, you are now using WM. You are, after all, holding information and reorganizing it into a new pattern.

If your friend tells you a phone number to write down, you rehearse it in your short-term memory until you find a pencil and paper. If, to satisfy a quirky curiosity, you add up the digits in the phone number, that math takes place in your WM.

If you're driving somewhere with your friend and you discover that the main road is under construction, you consider all your alternate routes in your WM.

Schools, in particular, place high demands on our students' WM. When learning to spell, students have to reorganize the letters they know into new combinations based on the words they hear. That's WM. When trying to understand mitosis, they re-sort chromosomes and organelles in their mental models of a cell. That's WM. When deciding who the antagonist is in *Macbeth*, students must realign the play's specific events to match up with a literary definition. Yup—WM.

In brief, students spend much of their academic day romping about in WM. To put it bluntly: WM is absolutely essential for all academic learning. Schools are, in effect, shrines built to honor successful WM achievement. No academic information gets into long-term memory except through WM. (Well, almost no academic information.)

We will spend the next three chapters investigating WM and its role in your classroom. Those memory demands look different in first grade and fifth grade; they look different in a Spanish class and a theology class. The suggestions that follow will be more helpful if you connect them immediately and directly to your own teaching world. Thus, to ensure that these chapters are as helpful to you as possible, you might pause right now for a minute to identify the WM tasks you ask your students to do.

Measuring Working Memory

Now that you've considered the tasks that require WM in your classroom, you probably want some idea of its capacity. Given that your students are constantly using their WM, how much room does it have? Exactly how many photographs does that end table hold?

The answer is—not very many.

To get a feel for the limitations of WM, try this three-step exercise:

Step one: Think of a 10-digit phone number that you know very well, and say those digits out loud. (Go ahead, say them. No one is looking.) Easy, right?

Step two: Now say those 10 digits backward. (No, really, try it.) Not so easy, but—after some initial hesitation—you can probably do this step readily enough.

Step three: Say the 10 digits backward again, but this time add 1 to the first digit, 2 to the second, 3 to the third, and so forth. (Push hard here: see if you can do this.)

This third task also feels difficult at first, but unlike the previous step, it quickly becomes impossible. Very few people succeed at this mental task.

And yet, this third step should not be all that difficult. You started with a number you know very well. You had a chance to practice saying it backward. And, adding single-digit numbers is first-grade arithmetic. But that arithmetic becomes next-to-impossible when you must also shuffle those ten digits about. You simply run out of cognitive space. (Your end table spilled the numbers under the credenza.)

Many people have an almost physical sensation when they experience WM overload. They describe it as "gears grinding" or "mental collapse" or "a brain thud." Teachers rarely experience this sensation in our classrooms, because we already know and understand the material we are teaching. The facts and concepts, in other words, are in our long-term memories, so we don't need to process them in WM. However, for students who don't yet have those ideas in long-term memory, those gears can grind far too often.

WM suffers from a second severe limitation: duration. Operations that we perform in WM fade away relatively quickly, typically in a matter of seconds. For example, just moments ago, you practiced saying a phone number backward. If you try to do so again right now, that task will be as laborious as it was the first time. When you changed from one cognitive task (saying numbers backward) to another (reading and contemplating the next sentences on the page), your WM buffers cleared out the old information to make room for the new.

Our knowledge of working memory's brevity comes from a fascinating, and tragic, case: the story of Henry Molaison (Corkin, 2013). In the 1950s, to cure debilitating epilepsy, H.M. (as he is best known) had specific brain regions removed. At the time, no one knew that those brain regions—the hippocampi—are essential for the formation of long-term declarative memory. As a result, Molaison lived for several decades without the ability to create such memories.

Molaison's case taught neuroscientists much of what we know about memory. For instance, he helped us understand the distinction between declarative and procedural memory. Without his hippocampi, H.M. couldn't explain how to get to the kitchen in his house; he didn't learn that information *declaratively*. However, when he wanted tea, he could go to the kitchen quite easily; he did learn that information *procedurally*. Procedural memories, after all, form in different regions of the brain, and so were not damaged by the surgery.

Lacking the ability to form long-term declarative memories, H.M. had to hold information in working memory. For instance, when he participated in memory studies, he had to remember specific instructions to follow. However, if a researcher gave instructions and then talked about something else even briefly, Molaison forgot those instructions—in fact, he forgot that he'd ever gotten them.

In short, decades of research and dozens of studies (including those into H.M.'s cognitive capacity) demonstrate that working memory is both small and short-lived.

Developing Working Memory

To recap: WM is both essential and very small. That's a terrible combination. (If you've got a wry sense of humor, you might note that it sounds like your school budget.)

Given this combination, teachers often ask an obvious question: What can we do to increase WM? Psychologists offer us two strategies.

Strategy #1: Wait. WM capacity naturally increases with age—at least through high school, and quite possibly through college.

To investigate this growth, Susan Gathercole's research team (Gathercole, Pickering, Ambridge, & Wearing, 2004) measured WM capacity in a number of different ways. When they studied students' ability to recall words, as shown in figure 1.1, WM capacity rose by 66 percent between the ages of 4 and 15. When they looked at the ability to manipulate digits or notice changes in visual patterns, those abilities increased roughly 150 percent. Clearly, WM grows during the ages that children are in school.

This graph requires an important reminder. The lines in figure 1.1 show *averages*, and individual students are never average (Rose, 2016). When Gathercole and Alloway (2008) calculated typical WM ranges, they found considerable variation at any given age. A seven-year-old at the tenth percentile has the WM capacity of a four-year-old. At the ninetieth percentile, a seven-year-old has the WM capacity of a ten-year-old. In other words, most children develop larger WM capacity as they grow, but they do not develop at the same rate. In a classroom of twenty students, you should expect to see quite a range.

Strategy #1 that psychologists offer to increase WM capacity: wait.

Strategy #2? Nothing. There is no workout regime that students can undertake, no diet they can follow, and no computer game they can play. WM

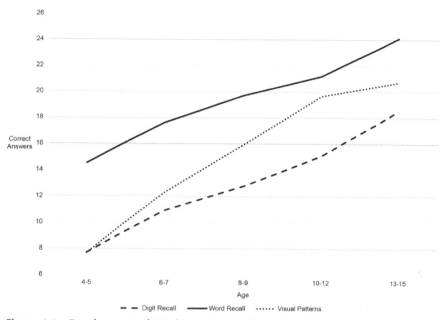

Figure 1.1 Development of Working Memory From Age 4 to 15. *Source*: **Based on Gathercole et al. (2008).**

develops on its own schedule, and—at least so far—we don't know how to create artificial improvement.

As you may know, this topic currently provokes substantial controversy. Several people claim to be able to increase WM capacity, and some sell products—typically computer programs—that purport to do so.

Their arguments do make some sense, at least on the surface. In recent decades, brain research has been energized by findings of neuroplasticity: that is, the discovery that brains ("neuro") can change ("plasticity") over time. For many decades, neuroscientists had believed that brains grew during childhood, and arrived at their final form relatively early. We now know that brains change throughout life, and that neurons can break old connections and form new ones. Given these findings of neuroplasticity, some argue, it simply makes sense that WM capacity should be able to change just like other kinds of brain function (Klingberg, 2009). To back up this general hypothesis, some researchers have found techniques that measurably increase WM capacity in psychology labs (Jaeggi, Buschkuehl, Jonides, & Perrig, 2008).

Sadly, however, these exciting plausibilities simply don't convert into useful classroom realities. Several studies make this point with increasing clarity. Melby-Lervåg and Hulme (2013) gathered twenty-three studies and analyzed their data. They found that although some of the training programs produced temporary effects, they did not reliably lead to long-term changes in learning. In the vocabulary of education research, that is, they did not "generalize": "The authors conclude that memory training programs appear to produce short-term, specific training effects that do not generalize ... Current findings cast doubt on both the clinical relevance of working memory training programs and their utility as methods of enhancing cognitive functioning in typically developing children and healthy adults" (Melby-Lervåg & Hulme, 2013, p. 270).

In another study (Dunning, Holmes, & Gathercole, 2013), researchers found that WM training made students better at other WM tests, but not at the academic work that matters in schools. As they put it:

> [Although] adaptive [working memory] training was associated with selective improvements in multiple [other] tests of working memory, [it showed] no evidence of changes in classroom analogues of activities that tax working memory, or any other cognitive assessments ... Thus the benefits of working memory training delivered in this way may not extend beyond structured working memory tasks. (Dunning, Holmes, & Gathercole, 2013, p. 2)

Many teachers, naturally enough, find these research conclusions disappointing. After all, we would love to enlarge our students' WM capacity, because that enhancement should help students learn. We also find these conclusions quite strange. If training programs can increase WM capacity, and WM facilitates learning, why don't these training programs facilitate greater learning? At present, we simply don't know the answer to this question. An analogy, however, might help.

As a volleyball coach, I notice that taller players have an advantage over shorter players. I therefore decide to see what happens if I make my players taller. I divide my team into three groups. Group A, the control group, I leave alone. I stretch Group B on the rack until they are 3 inches taller. I equip Group C with 6-inch stilts. I hypothesize that Group A players won't improve, Group B players will improve some, and Group C players will improve the most; after all, they gained the most height. Yet when I test my volleyball players, I find Group B got worse after being racked, and Group C is dramatically clumsier up on stilts. I conclude that although *naturally acquired* height benefits volleyball players, *artificially acquired* height does not. For this reason, I decide not to increase my players' height, but to help them play more skillfully with the height they already have.

So too with WM. The capacity our students develop naturally benefits their learning; any WM capacity artificially created by playing computer games does not. As a teacher, I should not try to stretch their WM. Instead, I should help them think and learn more effectively with the WM they already have. Happily, we know many strategies that teachers can use to do just that.

To recap: Research shows us that WM is *crucial* for learning, *small* in both capacity and duration, and *impervious to artificial improvement*. These three research conclusions lead to a resounding teaching conclusion—one that is central to this book: *We must become experts at teaching within our students' WM limits*. If we don't, they will feel the way you felt when you tried to add digits to your phone number. You felt irritated and confused, perhaps even embarrassed and angry. You certainly weren't in the learning zone. Because the task pushed past your WM capacity, mental photographs tumbled to the floor, and your brain was closed for business.

When I first learned about WM, twenty years after I had started teaching, I realized with horror how often my assignments made unreasonable demands on my students' WM capacity. I had thought they simply needed to work harder to succeed. But they didn't need to work harder; they needed more WM. And, of course, they could get more WM only by waiting several months. My students' difficulties resulted not from their own lack of effort, but from my own lack of knowledge about brains.

And yet, at the same time that WM research might make us regret many of our prior teaching practices, it also offers us immediate and practical guidance. However much we overloaded our students' end tables last year, we can lighten that load this year. By thinking about learning from a WM perspective, and by adopting specific classroom strategies, we can ensure that photos from long-term memory get sorted into beautiful new photo albums.

To take on this new WM perspective, we need to answer three essential questions:

1. How can I *anticipate* WM problems? As I look at a lesson plan, or a syllabus, or an assessment, or a classroom, how can I know where the WM difficulties might lurk?
2. How can I *identify* a WM problem when it occurs? Assuming that I don't anticipate all potential WM challenges, what will they look like when they happen? In medical language, what are the signs and symptoms of WM overload?
3. How can I *solve* WM problems? Once I anticipate them (question #1), how do I prevent them from occurring? Once I identify them (question #2), how do I fix them?

Teachers can be tempted to skip the first two questions and jump right to the third. We naturally like practicing solutions more than we like dwelling on potential errors. Yet those two introductory questions make the third one possible. Unless we can anticipate problem before they happen, or spot them

Anticipate WM Overload	Identify WM Overload
Solutions to WM Problems	

Figure 1.2   Three Working Memory Questions.

when they do, we will never know when to use all the solutions that research supports.

Chapter 2 explores the first two questions, helping teachers to anticipate and identify WM problems. Chapter 3 offers research-informed strategies to help us solve those problems. In other words, we will revisit and fill in figure 1.2 in chapters 2 and 3. To conclude part I, chapter 4 summarizes these chapters with a specific classroom example, and then answers frequently asked questions about WM in schools.

Chapter Two

Two Burning Questions

In chapter 1, as we considered photographs strewn across a table, we realized that teachers need to focus keenly on our students' working memory. After all, information can't get into long-term memory—that is, photographs can't get into new photo albums—if we don't help students manage this cognitive process. Students need WM to contemplate Boyle's law, make sense of the word "pulchritude," and multiply fractions; alas, they just don't have very much WM to do that work. Doubly alas: we can't make it any bigger.

In chapter 2, we will consider two of the three questions that teachers need answered. First, now that we understand the profound dangers of WM overload, how can we anticipate it? As we look at lesson plans, syllabi, assessments, and classroom practices, how can we know where WM problems might arise?

Second, what does WM overload look like when it happens? Only the rare student will say: "Mr. Watson, that question went beyond my WM limits. Could you lower those cognitive demands please?" In the absence of such feedback, how will we know that students have a WM problem—rather than, say, a motivational problem? Or, a long-term memory problem?

ANTICIPATING WORKING MEMORY OVERLOAD

You've got a stack of papers on your desk: lesson plans, seating charts, quizzes, syllabi, project rubrics, and class rules. You know that, given the narrow confines of WM capacity, some tasks on those papers threaten your students' cognitive capabilities. Where should you look? It seems daunting and impractical to rehearse every moment of the upcoming week's classes to find those hot spots. How can you narrow your focus to the most probable culprits?

Happily, with some guidance from researchers, we can identify the most common ways that academic work weighs on WM capacity.

Too Much Information

In our imperfect analogy, WM overload happens when the number of photographs exceeds the capacity of the end table. To anticipate WM overload, we can first look for those moments when students must work with an unusually large number of photos: that is, when they process lots of new information.

New Information

Imagine, for example, that you plan to teach a summer school course in "20th Century American History through Music." As your students learn about "The Charleston" and "Brother, Can You Spare a Dime," "R-E-S-P-E-C-T," and "(Four Dead in) Ohio," they will absorb not only the musical information that intrinsically inspires them, but also the historical information that sometimes leaves them oddly indifferent. You're working with an eager intern, and you offer up an important question: How should you spend your first class? You tell your intern to come back in a week with some ideas.

Your intern—wanting to impress—gets back to you immediately: "I've been looking over the syllabus, and I see that they've got a lot of musical vocabulary to learn: *syncopation* and *downbeat* and *crescendo* and *plunger mute*, and a couple of dozen more. They really can't do the thoughtful analysis we want without knowing that vocabulary. Since our students won't have done any homework for this first class, we can use it to teach them all that terminology. With that chore crossed off our to-do list, we can really dig into the material. In fact, I've got a great idea for introducing Ragtime on day two ..."

Your eager intern's idea suffers from more than one problem. In the first place, it sounds like a dreadfully boring lesson plan. Worse than boring, it will surely be an ineffective lesson plan because it will utterly overwhelm your students' WM. Depending on their age, grade, and prior musical knowledge, they might be able to absorb four or six or eight new musical terms. But dozens? Not a chance. You might be able to go over them all, and they might be polite enough on the first day to pretend to pay attention. But they simply don't have enough space in WM to connect so many new words and concepts to their current store of musical knowledge. Their end tables will splinter into kindling.

When a practice sentence in Spanish requires several fresh vocabulary words, when a math problem includes both multiplication and exponents, when students must spell words with six letters instead of five—if that level of cognitive challenge is unusual for your students, it may well go beyond their WM capacity. The specific limitations will vary depending on your students and the material you teach—that's why you made a list of your classroom's WM demands a few minutes ago. But the general rule is clear: When you present more new information than your students typically handle, be on the lookout for WM overload.

Un/related Information

The amount of new information matters, but other features matter as well.

Here's an example. A teacher might instruct his students to write a story that includes four elements: a brother, a sister, a house, and a pet. Or, perhaps the story must include a sea urchin, a farthing, a barn, and a tea cozy.

Although both lists include the same number of elements—that is, they have the same amount of new information—they pose dramatically different WM loads. When you think of a sister, after all, that piece of the story reminds you of a brother. Those siblings automatically make you think about a house and a pet. In the second story, however, nothing about a sea urchin prompts you to think about a barn, and neither of those typically has a tea cozy nearby. For this reason, *unrelated information* can pose a higher WM burden than related information. Thus, as teachers scan our lesson plans for too much information, we should also look for dramatically unrelated information.

In some unusual circumstances, information that is highly related can also pose a WM challenge (Gathercole & Alloway, 2008). If students must remember the words "tall, fall, mall, wall, Saul, Paul, Gaul, and haul," the very similarity of those words can ramp up the cognitive load of this task—especially if they must exclude the words "ball, call, awl, and maul." For this reason, the Battle of Gettysburg poses a slightly greater WM challenge if students must distinguish between *Cemetery Ridge* and *Seminary Ridge*. The similar sounds of those words make them harder to distinguish than, for instance, *Lexington* and *Concord*. AP Psychology teachers know that students struggle to distinguish between *authoritative* and *authoritarian* parenting styles (except, perhaps, when they're experiencing them).

Combining Information

WM both holds onto pieces of information and combines that information. Teachers must be careful to monitor the pieces and the combining. Even if the amount of information seems manageable, requiring new combinations might overwhelm cognitive processes (Willingham, 2009).

In my biology class, for example, we have spent the last few weeks studying various systems of human anatomy: the skeletal system, the muscular system, the endocrine system, and so forth. We've devoted quite a lot of class time and homework to these topics, and so none of this information is new anymore. To help my students prepare for an upcoming test, I ask them the following question: "Imagine I spend a minute breathing in and out of a small paper bag. What will happen in my kidneys?"

Because I am—in this example—a biology teacher, the answer to this question is perfectly clear. Breathing into the paper bag will raise the CO_2 concentration in my lungs. The lungs, of course, connect to the circulatory system, and so the CO_2 concentration in my blood will also rise. And when my kidneys filter the blood, they will recognize the change in pH balance created by the increased CO_2, and will do their kidney magic to restore pH to its proper level. Because I have studied biology for so long, the connections among these various systems come easily to me.

For my students, none of this information is new. However, this chain of logic combines old knowledge in new ways and therefore poses quite a stiff WM challenge. As novices in biology, students struggle to combine more than two or three steps in new and unfamiliar ways. When they hear my question about breathing and kidneys, they probably start wondering frantically if they missed a paragraph in the textbook that explains how kidneys react to brown paper. They will need WM relief before they can think through this multistep logical chain.

This particular limitation makes it especially challenging to develop effective assessments. On the one hand, we often want our students to combine information in new ways to demonstrate their understanding of the material. After all, if they simply repeat what we did in class, they are parroting, not learning. On the other hand, if the WM requirements of those new combinations go beyond their cognitive limits, then the test doesn't measure their understanding. Instead, it measures our own misunderstanding of WM.

One test in my own teaching career stands out for this reason—and not in a good way. On a vocabulary test, I instructed my students to complete sentences using words from the lesson they had just studied. In addition, I told them to describe the people in those sentences using vocabulary words from previous lessons. They had, by that time in the year, studied well over hundred words. This test, in other words, asked students to flip through dozens of old photographs—and they simply ran out of end table. They complained quite bitterly about the test, and they were right to do so. If I had known about WM limitations, I would have seen right away that I was asking them to make too many connections between too many words and too many new sentences.

Creative and Critical Combinations

Because creativity is one of humanity's most admirable abilities, many researchers have studied this often-puzzling capability. Researcher Shelley

Carson has proposed an insightful and useful model to understand creativity—a model that includes WM.

Carson focuses on one person's ability to think about the world differently than others do: a capacity called *cognitive disinhibition*. To measure cognitive disinhibition, a researcher gives a participant an everyday object and asks for a list of all the ways it might be used. If I give you two bricks, you might say that bricks can be used to build a wall. This answer is true, but not at all uncommon. In this case, you have not demonstrated much cognitive disinhibition.

However, the bricks might strike you as a solution to a problem you have at home: your pool float is so heavy that it's cumbersome to take out of the pool. Holding those two bricks, you might decide to throw lots of bricks into the pool to raise its water level. You can easily slide the float out, and then remove the bricks to return the water to its appropriate level. This use for bricks is quite atypical, and so this answer will raise your cognitive disinhibition score. (It will also encourage the research team to invite themselves over for poolside margaritas.)

Carson (2011) has found that unusually creative people score high on tests of both *cognitive disinhibition and WM*. This finding makes sense: to be creative, you must both see the world in atypical ways (with your cognitive disinhibition) and have enough cognitive work room (your WM) to do something with that vision.

This research insight has important classroom implications.

Often, in class, we ask our students to do comfortably familiar work. In order to automate basic processes, we want them to repeat the same cognitive steps with only slight variations. Once they learn how to solve for three variables using three equations, they practice that procedure with multiple different variables. Once they have learned how to distinguish between similes and metaphors, we have them review several poems to practice this skill. This kind of work is important, but it does not stand out for its creativity.

At other times, we ask our students to move beyond the comfortable and the familiar so that they might stretch their cognitive skills. These stretches might be explicitly creative: writing a poem, composing a song, and performing a scene from an August Wilson play. Or, such stretches might come under the heading of critical thinking: imagining the specific evolutionary pressures that caused two species to break off from a common ancestor, or devising a platform for a new political party that will appeal to young voters.

Whether we call these cognitive leaps *creativity* or *critical thinking*, we must be aware that this part of the assignment will tax WM above and beyond its surface features. No matter how well my students know current party platforms, the creative effort to conjure a new one will create an extra level of WM challenge.

In sum, to anticipate WM overload, look for that part of a lesson plan, homework assignment, or assessment that includes lots of new, unrelated information, or new and creative combinations of information.

Beware the Dark Side, Luke

As Anakin Skywalker could tell you, the Force is a good thing until it's a bad thing. So too with some of our cherished classroom habits. Many of our teacherly routines help students learn, until those same routines abruptly produce WM problems. Three kinds of classroom practice in particular may cross over to the Dark Side.

Instructions

For our students to learn new processes, we often ask them to do something. And to be sure they do that something correctly, we give them instructions. If they do the right steps in the right order, that mental activity helps them learn.

And yet, instructions also take a cognitive toll. Students must often hold instructions in WM. Those instructions therefore reduce the capacity that students have left over to learn.

If you've been teaching for even a year or two, you can probably recall a time your students simply stopped functioning when given perfectly simple instructions. You told your second graders to stand up, push in their chairs, take a book to the carpet, and sit quietly. A chaos of questions enveloped you. You asked your tenth graders to take out some paper and complete the graphic organizer you had started on the board. Bedlam. In a middle school science class, you told your budding researchers how to set up a slide on a microscope. Throughout the room, you heard heads hitting lab tables as their cognitive gears ground to a halt.

Depending on your comfort with computers, you may experience this overload yourself when hearing instructions about some new program or another. Someone—invariably a younger, exasperated someone—tells you to highlight these words, right click on that menu, select the third option, and toggle over to plasma mode, unless you're using a Mac, in which case the instructions go in the reverse order. Because you haven't yet located the words to highlight, your WM collapses under the weight of all those steps.

A group of researchers led by Susan Gathercole has investigated the relationship between WM capacity and the ability to follow classroom instructions. They asked five- and six-year-olds to perform an increasingly complex series of tasks: for example, to "touch the red pencil, THEN pick up the blue ruler and put it in the black box" (Gathercole, Durling, Evans, Jeffcock, & Stone, 2008, p. 1029). As you can see, this study design focused on the very objects that students are likely to find in their classrooms. Gathercole's team found, as they had hypothesized, that students with higher WM levels were able to perform more instructions correctly.

One further point about instructions. Typically, classroom instructions tell students what they should do right now. Occasionally, they tell students what they should do later. Instructions that are to be performed over a period of time are especially popular on the Death Star. If we tell our students to do step one right now, step two if they get a particular result, and step three if they get a different result, they face a steep WM climb. They have to hold onto these instructions for several minutes, and they have to remember the conditions under which to follow each one. Remembering to do something in the future drains WM with grim effectiveness (Smith, 2003).

In all these ways, seemingly helpful instructions might turn into WM detriments.

Choices

Students typically find choices motivating (Deci & Ryan, 2000), and so it may seem strange to suggest that choices have a Dark Side. And yet, if you've spent a stunned three minutes standing in the toothpaste aisle of a drugstore, you know that choices can overwhelm WM. After all, as you compared the price, hue, and flavor of one toothpaste to dozens of others, all that mental juggling took place in WM.

Students face this danger particularly when they're stuck with a problem. If my student says, "I know that this is an awkward sentence but I don't know how to make it better," I might respond with a helpful list: "You could choose a stronger verb, reduce the number of prepositional phrases, use parallelism to strengthen the logic of the argument, or subordinate the quotation in an appositive." That list, in fact, has taken years of teaching to develop, and I might be proud of each suggestion. However, by providing so many options to a student whose cognition is already under stress, I am likely not to solve the problem, but to push my student into Lord Vader's arms.

This potential overload can, for the best of reasons, sneak up in assessments and homework assignments. We might, for example, give students choices on a test: they can pick three problems from the first page, one graph on the second page, and then make up their own word problem on the third. We might give them eight or ten essay options for the Silk Road unit, the last being "make up your own topic." While this salad bar approach might seem cognitively healthy, it might also add pressure to an already overstressed WM.

Technology

On the one hand, technology can help students learn in dozens of ways. Flashcard programs simplify vocabulary learning. Word processors reduce the strain of writing and revising essays. Once carefully sifted, information from the Internet can keep knowledge current, vital, and occasionally fun. Teachers and learners have many reasons to thank the gods of technology.

On the other hand, technology routinely threatens to overload WM capacity.

Many programs that students use to accomplish their school work can overwhelm beginners with choices. For example, if students decide to make a class presentation using PowerPoint (or iMovie, or a Google Doc), they might well be distracted from their presentation's content by all the program's options. Should they outline the title text with bright magenta? Which transition should they choose to advance from one slide to the next? Should the text fade in or fly in or wipe in? PowerPoint offers all these choices, and surrounds them with literally hundreds more. While students use their WM capacity to think through their ideas, they must also rely on WM to manage the pull-down-menu-Palooza.

Skilled users of these programs know which options to use and how to think through their choices. For experts, thus, such complicated programs may not yield WM problems. For beginners, who have only just begun to explore the possibilities, WM collapse may be a click away.

Technology also routinely tempts our students to multitask. In one stunning Canadian study (Karsenti & Fievez, 2013), 6,055 of 6,057 high-school students said that "distraction" was the biggest problem caused by using iPads in class. (It would be fascinating to talk with those two undistracted students.)

To explore the effect of this distraction, one study investigated two questions: one predictable and the other surprising. In the study's predictable phase, Faria Sana asked college students to watch a forty-five-minute lecture on meteorology and take notes on their laptops (Sana, Weston, & Cepeda, 2013). She then gave them a quiz on the lecture to see how much they learned about clouds and thunderstorms.

A second group of students watched the same lecture, again taking notes on their computers. However, these students were connected to the Internet, and given several minitasks: for instance, to find information about the television schedule for that evening. When these students took the same quiz, they scored 11 percent lower. Predictably enough, students distracted by their Internet multitasking did not learn as much as their monotasking peers.

The second half of Sana's study then investigated a more surprising question: What effect did Internet surfing have on those *seated behind* the surfers? Two new groups of Sana's students watched the meteorology lecture. Half sat behind peers taking hand-written notes; the other half sat behind peers who were switching from laptop notes to Facebook to email to—presumably—Buzzfeed listicles. Even though the second group did not multitask themselves, their scores were 17 percent lower than the scores of students who sat behind handwriters.

In both these cases, technology created the opportunity for multitasking—that is, rapid processing of unrelated information streams. As noted above, unrelated information poses an even greater WM tax than related information, and so we should expect this Internet-induced back-n-forth to hamper our students' cognition.

For both these reasons, teachers need to be thoughtful when introducing technology to a lesson plan or an assessment. The vital question: How can our students get the benefits of a particular technology without losing cognitive resources to WM overload?

As you review your upcoming lesson plans, you should look both for potential IT-choice overload and for the typically helpful technology that can—in the hands of a Sith Lord—endanger your students' WM.

That Sinking Feeling

Inspired by a workshop we attended last spring, our teaching team has developed a new unit to kick off our Junior English curriculum: the Three Authors Project. Our students will go to the library and choose novels by three authors with dramatically different writing styles. And here's the fun part: they will then transform a passage from one author into the style of another. That is, they'll take—say—a Jane Austen paragraph, and rewrite it to sound like Charles Chesnutt. And then they'll take a Chesnutt passage and revise it with Kurt Vonnegut's voice.

To ensure that they ground this literary adventure in a solid understanding of language, our students will describe these transformations using the grammar concepts they studied last year. In other words, they'll talk about rewriting a Vonnegut passage with Austen's free indirect discourse, or Hemingway's lack of subordination, or Fitzgerald's parallel prepositional phrases.

This project offers all sorts of benefits. First, it motivates students by allowing them freedom and giving them responsibility. Rather than answering required questions about a required text, our students get to choose their own adventure: the freshly discovered authors who enchant them, the passages that will be fun to rewrite, and the stylistic experiments that feel most energizing. Rather than mechanically following routine instructions, they take charge of their own learning.

Second, it allows our students to construct their own understanding of the material. Once they try to write as Toni Morrison writes, they will read her shocking prose with fresh appreciation for its adventurousness. Once they try to leave out as much as Raymond Carver leaves out, they will be wiser—when reading other Carver stories—in completing his gaps and silences. And because they will have a chance to use grammatical terminology in a meaningful way, unlike those dreary back-of-the-chapter exercises, they will truly appreciate its usefulness. When they make these connections and draw these conclusions on their own—after genuine cognitive effort—the learning that results will be more meaningful and enduring

In short, by motivating our students to construct knowledge for themselves, the Three Authors Project may well create deep and lasting understanding of this material. They will, at last, start thinking like English scholars.

And yet, as we looked over this plan with WM limitations in mind, our Junior English team started to get a sinking feeling in the pit of our syllabus.

- *Does this project give our students too much new information?* Well, the school's library hosts literally hundreds of novels by dozens of authors.
- *Does it ask them to combine that information in creative new ways?* Creative new combinations are the very goal of this assignment.
- *Does it include lots of intricate instructions—some of which are to be completed later?* Well, in order to be clear about all the project's multistep complexities, the assignment sheet goes on for pages.
- *Does it offer lots of choices?* Ahem. We can't really count how many.

In other words, although intended to help students "create deep and lasting understanding of this material," the Three Authors Project might very well crash their WM. And, as we now know, a broken WM prevents any information from getting into long-term memory.

Teaching with projects is much prized these days, and it's easy to see why. Given the joyless drudgery that we often hear about in schools, teachers naturally want to make learning enduring and inspiring. As noted above, the Platonic Ideal of a project can motivate students and help them learn deeply.

For many teachers, our most thrilling school memories resulted from such open-ended assignments. I myself can talk at epic length about my journey to the Rare Book Collection of the Cleveland Public Library. There, to my great surprise, a primary source for a history project turned out to be written in French. In that pre-Internet moment, I borrowed a dictionary from the desk and—translating giddily—felt like Shackleton questing toward the South Pole.

And yet, as we consider the essential elements of such projects, we can see that WM perils are often built right in. Project pedagogies typically recommend giving students more information than they really need, so that they can learn to distinguish the useful information from the trivial. (For this reason, the Three Authors Project has students choose books from library shelves—rather than from, say, a short list provided by the teacher.) Alas, a superabundance of new information is the very first potential WM danger discussed above.

Project pedagogies typically ask students to construct knowledge by putting together substantial bodies of information in novel ways. (Hence, students working with Three Authors take events from one novel and write about them in the voice of another.) Yet here again, this demand for many new combinations can overwhelm cognitive capacities.

Wanting students to have room to fail before they succeed, project pedagogies often discourage teachers from providing support. Teachers should let students work out difficulties on their own in order for them to learn more deeply. (To compensate for this silence, the Three Authors assignment sheet offers highly detailed instructions to guide students along the way.) Unfortunately, extra instructions add to the accumulating WM burden of the project.

A famous study, first published in 1973, helps explain why these kinds of projects can simultaneously be so exciting to teachers and so daunting for students.

William Chase and Herbert Simon wanted to understand the influence of *expertise* on perception. Specifically, they wanted to know if expert chess players see chessboards differently than do chess beginners (Chase & Simon, 1973). This question, on its face, sounds rather strange. We would expect that all people *see* the same chessboard, and that beginners and experts *think* differently about what they see. But Chase and Simon hypothesized that beginners and experts literally see different chessboards. They differ not only in cognition, but also in perception.

To test their hypothesis, Chase and Simon had experts and beginners look at pieces set up on a chessboard, and then recreate what they had seen on a blank chessboard of their own. When the original chess pieces were randomly distributed—that is, not a meaningful part of a chess game—experts and beginners were equally successful at accomplishing this task. In other words, when experts did not benefit from their chess knowledge, they saw the same physical reality that beginners did.

However, when the pieces were set up in the middle of an actual chess game, experts gained a striking advantage. After five seconds, beginners placed about four pieces correctly. Experts quadrupled that score, placing almost sixteen pieces correctly. When they could draw on their chess expertise, experts no longer saw the same world that the chess beginners did. Perception works differently for experts.

Psychologists have researched different kinds of expertise, and regularly draw this same conclusion. For example, when Tracy Hogan surveyed literature on teacher expertise, she and her team found a similar pattern in schools (Hogan, Rabinowitz, & Craven, 2003). Novice teachers typically focus on the students directly in front of them. Expert teachers, on the other hand, have much better peripheral vision, especially when problems in student behavior occur off to the side. In teaching as in chess, novices and experts literally see different realities.

Presumably, experts see more because their expertise allows them to recognize meaningful patterns. A novice chess player sees a pawn here and a rook there, whereas an expert sees well-known strategies: one player is using the Anna's Dragon gambit to attack the second player's Gracious Goalie defense. Both novices and experts have the same underlying perceptual capacity. But experts' ability to process meaningful groups of pieces allows them to absorb more information.

Alas, the Three Authors Project requires an expert's perception. As English teachers, our team can easily see the meaningful patterns necessary to reduce WM load. We know dozens of authors with distinctive prose styles. We know how the grammar terminology we've been studying helps describe those differences. We would thoroughly enjoy revising Charles Dickens to sound like Gertrude Stein. If you sent us to the library to undertake this project, we would race toward the stacks with a bright-eyed glee.

Our students, however, resemble beginners more than experts when it comes to knowledge of English literature. They are unlikely to remember different authors' prose styles on their own. They find grammar sentences from the textbook a significant challenge; it's very unlikely that they can recognize how Fitzgerald's prepositional phrases set him apart from Joyce's nonce words. Standing in the library—glumly facing hundreds of books—they will pluck down one volume, scan a random page, replace it on the shelf, and hope the next one offers a more promising paragraph. Because ... what are they supposed to be doing again?

As beginners, our students simply cannot sort all these possibilities into meaningful patterns. Their WM systems will almost certainly collapse under the weight of choices—especially because they're not allowed to ask us for guidance. However much we would like them to construct new knowledge on their own, they don't yet perceive information as experts do, and so will be overwhelmed by possibilities.

Do WM limitations therefore require teachers to forgo project pedagogies altogether?

Many researchers who have studied project-based learning and problem-based learning have found reasons to doubt their effectiveness (Alfieri, Brooks, Aldrich, & Tenenbaum, 2011; Mayer, 2004). Their real-world data, combined with a scientific understanding of WM, make a strong case to set these approaches aside.

At the same time, many teachers believe quite passionately that they have great success with project pedagogies. And at least one student—standing in the Rare Book Collection at the very top of Cleveland's library—has reveled in the freedom and insight they allow. What, then, is the right balance to strike? To project or not to project?

The answer to this question, as is so often the case, lies with individual teachers as we think about our students, our schools, our curriculum, and our approaches to teaching. To find our answer wisely, we should keep several important points in mind.

First, as is always true when thinking about science, we must be clear on terminology. These WM concerns arise about very specific project pedagogies: those that encourage students to handle lots of information with little teacher involvement. The word "project," as more traditionally understood in schools, need not alarm us. When students are making posters or identifying trees in a nearby park, such projects might energize learning quite helpfully. Like everything else that happens in schools, such traditional projects can be good or bad. Teachers should scrutinize them for potential WM overload as we scrutinize all our assignments. But we need not abandon projects entirely.

Second, some teachers find great success with project-based learning and problem-based learning. Given their students' enthusiasm (and perhaps their grades), these teachers zealously champion this approach to teaching. If you find yourself in this category, you need not fall unquestioningly into line. Teachers should listen to the findings of psychologists and neuroscientists, but we need not ignore our own experience.

This point comes with essential caveats: We must be honest with ourselves about the definition of "success." Have our students in fact learned what we wanted them to learn? How do we know? What measurement are we using? Are we being rigorous with ourselves and our students about their understanding?

Equally important, we should deliberately look for WM problem spots. Where have our students struggled the most during the project? Did those struggles lead ultimately to greater learning, or did they impede it?

Teachers who explore these last questions often find that they have been solving WM problems without realizing it. In the language of project pedagogies, they have been using more "guided" discovery learning than "pure" discovery learning (Mayer, 2004). When we review WM solutions in chapter 3, you may recognize strategies that you have already employed to reduce excess cognitive load.

Third, students who have achieved some level of expertise may do quite well with project-based learning assignments. To decide on your students' level of expertise, you should look for three characteristics.

A. Students should have spent a considerable amount of time doing these particular tasks. No one achieves expertise quickly.
B. They should be completely comfortable with the specialized vocabulary necessary to do the project. For example, students still trying to identify

various pieces of lab equipment will need WM for that task, and will have little left over for discovery about cell walls.

C. They should be fluent in seeing connections and patterns. Chess experts see that this bishop protects that rook, which prevents an opponent's knight from moving to that open square. So too, your students should be able to make new connections and derive situation-specific inferences—even in situations they have not seen before.

The research project that took me to the Rare Book Collection allowed me to create my own knowledge by managing large amounts of new material—some of it written in French! In other words, it sounds like discovery learning at its purest.

And yet, I had years of experience in the underlying parts of this work. I had written several research papers my junior and senior years of high school; these routines were quite familiar to me. I had spent several weeks learning about this specific research topic, and so I had clear cognitive frameworks for the new information that I was learning. And I had been studying French for six years. Well prepared by excellent teachers, equipped with a sturdy dictionary, I knew just how to make my way through this new text. My relative expertise in several parts of this process made the discovery part of the learning possible. Without all that hard-earned knowledge, I might well have slunk out of the Rare Book Collection in glum confusion.

In sum, project pedagogies sound very appealing. When we give students lots of information and lots of freedom to learn by trial and error, the meaning they construct should be both exciting and enduring. At the same time, the fierce logic of WM—its importance and its limitations—encourages teachers to adopt this approach cautiously, skillfully, and even skeptically. We must rely on our judgment and experience, and on the helpful research that science can offer, to find the best project methods. In particular, although project pedagogies may create exciting—even thrilling—experiences for budding experts, they may overwhelm WM for beginners.

Asleep at the Working Memory Switch

Human cognitive capacities change over the course of our lives, and they also change over the course of a day. As will be discussed in the Attention section, our ability to exert self-control can be depleted during our waking hours (Baumeister & Tierney, 2011). So, too, with WM. Experience and common sense suggest that tired students struggle with WM tasks.

When contemplating a lesson plan, therefore, we should give some thought to the time of day. If two sections of juniors are taking the same test, students who take it at 7:30 am are at a distinct disadvantage compared with those who take it at 10:00 am. Combining letters into new words will be harder for first graders before their nap than after.

This cognitive principle shapes our ideas for homework assignments as well. Students who undertake a WM-intensive assignment late at night may well lack the cognitive resources they had earlier in the day. In other words, we should notice when take-home assignments include unusually high WM demands, and develop specific strategies to help students manage them.

This chapter started by asking the first of our three questions: How can we anticipate potential WM overload? So far, we have seen that new information, unrelated information, and creative and critical combinations of information might raise WM demands too steeply. We have seen that several useful teaching tools—instructions, choices, and technology—have a potential Dark Side. We know that some project pedagogies encourage strategies that weigh on WM. And, we have recalled that tired students don't think well. Figure 2.1 summarizes these points.

As you look at those lesson plans and assessments and syllabi stacked on your desk, therefore, you can start by looking for these elements. Where does a test ask students to combine more new information than usual? Where does your description of a lab technique include too many instructions—especially instructions that take place over time? Where does a project require an expert's perception to manage the cognitive load? At what time will your

Anticipate WM Overload	Identify WM Overload

1. Too much information:
    new, un/related, combined
2. The Dark Side of the Force:
    instructions, choices, technology
3. Project pedagogies
4. Time of day	

Solutions to WM Problems	

Figure 2.1 **Anticipating Working Memory Overload.**

students be doing this especially challenging WM task? Answering these questions will help us anticipate the WM challenges we have previously over-looked. Now that we can anticipate them, the solutions presented in chapter 3 will be all the more practical.

IDENTIFYING WORKING MEMORY OVERLOAD

Our second burning question: What does WM overload look like when it happens?

To some degree, this question might sound like a pessimist's query. We have just spent several pages learning how to anticipate WM overload, and so it seems unlikely that we will ever need to identify it. Having scoured lesson plans for new combinations, having simplified instructions on tomor-row's test, and having lightened the cognitive load for the creative part of next week's homework, we might feel confident that our students will never experience WM problems again.

Yet the question isn't pessimistic, but practical. In the first place—as all teachers know—plans go astray. Helmuth von Moltke (the elder) observed that no battle plan survives contact with the enemy. So too, no lesson plan survives contact with the daily revelry of school. A do-now exercise might prompt an unexpected question and a lengthy answer. Our exploration of the first law of thermodynamics might take less time than anticipated. Teaching always requires inspired improvisation, and our improv might very well take students into WM thickets.

Second, as noted in chapter 1, students in our classes most likely have quite a wide range of WM capacity. High-school freshmen might juggle cognitive variables with the agility of college freshmen, or the relative ponderousness of sixth graders. An exercise that energizes high-WM students might well daunt low-WM students. As we negotiate our way along that spectrum, we should be on the lookout for the signs and symptoms of cognitive collapse.

Third, paradoxically, a class that never threatens WM might well be short-changing its students. Just as weight lifters need to be working at the limits of their strength to build muscle, so too our students should be lift-ing heavy cognitive weights. Most of us, as we search for the right level of challenge, will occasionally go too far. (A teacher who can push students exactly to—but never beyond—their WM limits has rare gifts indeed.) As long as we promptly recognize this mistake and pull back cognitive demands, these occasional stresses cause less harm than never having pushed in the first place. We should, in other words, see occasional WM struggles as a sign of appropriately demanding pedagogy. (By the way: the brain-as-muscle analogy is useful, but has as many imperfections as the

WM-as-end-table analogy. In important ways, brains behave very differently from muscles.)

How, then, do students behave when we overtax WM? What diagnostic criteria should we look for? The three answers below may feel both surprising and uncomfortably familiar.

46 × 38 = Despair

In today's class, you read a twelve-word sentence out loud and instructed your students to write it down. To accomplish even this simple task, your students had to *remember* all the words you read. If they didn't keep all twelve words in mind, after all, they would fail by the second or third word. Simultaneously, students had to *process* each word as they wrote it down. They had to recall how to spell "tomorrow," how to form the possessive of "women," and how to distinguish among "their," "there," and "they're."

Any time that students hold and process information, they are using WM. If you see them fail at either the *holding* or the *processing*, you are watching WM collapse.

For example, most adults know that 7 × 5 = 35. But if you multiply 46 × 38 in your head, you must first process specific pieces of that equation (6 × 8 = 48), then hold the 8 in the ones place and the 4 in the tens place while you process next piece of the equation (6 × 3 = 18). If at this stage in the process, you can't remember that you must add 4 to the 18, then your WM gave up on the holding. If—because you were concentrating on all that holding—you multiplied 6 × 3 and got 24, then your WM couldn't process information correctly. In either case, the dual demands of holding and processing overwhelmed your WM.

What does this failure look like in class? In the write-down-the-sentence example, a struggling student won't be able to *hold* the complete sentence while *processing* each word. If she can't manage processing, then she will misspell a word, or skip a word (or, perhaps, write one word twice). If she can't continue holding, then she will lose track of the sentence, which might very well turn into nonsense.

If a chemistry student attempts to set electrons in electron configuration shells, she must both process each individual electron and remember the complex sequence of electrons she has already placed. When she runs out of WM capacity, she won't be able to place the next electron correctly. When attempting to form the subjunctive in French, students must keep track of several different rules—when to use it, how to form it—and apply them all correctly. If these translators-to-be apply the subjunctive to a factual statement, or use the future perfect form instead, they've gone outside their ability to hold and process.

We can also see this remembering-while-processing error in classroom routines. If a student has to follow several instructions, he must remember them all while processing each one. If this student skips a crucial instruction, or gives up in frustration with the whole project, he might very well have lost the ability to process and remember that list. Likewise, if a student raises her hand but can't remember her question when you call on her, you're witnessing a WM problem. She has to remember her question and simultaneously process the information going on in the class around her. When that dual load becomes too much, she can no longer remember her question.

As we look for these remembering-while-processing errors, we should distinguish between individual problems and group problems. If you have several students in a row who raise their hands and then forget their questions, you may very well have gone beyond the WM capacity of your entire class. So too if only a few of them can follow all the instructions for an assignment, or if no one can formulate the subjective correctly. In these cases, you most likely need to reduce the WM demands overall.

However, if you have only one student making these kinds of mistakes, your mission is quite different—although an equally interesting challenge. In this second case, you want to support this individual student's WM without oversimplifying the task for all the other students. All the strategies that we will discuss in chapter 3 might be used for the whole class if you see a general problem or for individuals if you see only a student or two struggling.

Because this symptom looks different in each of our classrooms, it might be helpful for you to pause again and consider your specific teaching context. When you think back to the most recent class you taught, where did that lesson plan ask students to process and remember at the same time? Which students struggled with that task? What, specifically, did those students do? Can you think of their behavior as a consistent sign of WM overload in your classroom? Take a few minutes to think through and write down your own specific answers to these questions.

Atypical Distractibility

Teachers typically think of distractibility as an attention problem, not a WM problem. After all, we often respond to our students' distraction by reminding them to "pay attention!" (The reasons that this strategy rarely works, or works only temporarily, will be a central topic of chapter 5.) However, distractibility may instead be a sign of WM overload. This counter-intuitive statement requires some exploration.

If I ask you to alphabetize the last names of the five most recent U.S. presidents, your WM gathers knowledge from your long-term memory: who those presidents are, how to spell their names, and the order of the alphabet. You must also draw on information from the outside world: the instructions that I just gave you. How does that information get from the outside world into your WM? That's what your attention system does.

The precise mechanisms by which these steps happen are extremely complicated and not yet fully understood (Fougnie, 2008; Kiyonaga & Egner, 2013). But conceptually, the basic outline is clear. To ensure that only the most pertinent information comes in from the outside world, WM and attention systems collaborate to filter out the useless and focus on the relevant.

For instance, when you alphabetized the names of U.S. presidents, your attentional system filtered out needless information so you could focus on the instructions. Because they were not important to your cognitive task, your attentional system didn't register the color in the carpet or the ache in your left elbow.

However, if the WM system is overloaded, it can't play its part in this complex process. As a result, attention systems filter less effectively, and students become increasingly distractible. In other words, the behavior of our distracted students may be telling us that their current task is overtaxing WM.

Of course, teachers know that all students are distractible. We need not interpret every moment of distraction as a sign of WM doom. Instead, we should look for *atypical* distractibility. If this group of students usually gets right down to work Tuesday second period, and yet this particular Tuesday they are scampering around the room like giddy otters, this unusual behavior might well suggest that their WM capacity is under strain.

Symptom of WM overload #1: difficulty remembering while processing. Symptom #2: atypical distractibility.

Catastrophic Failure

We had an excellent English class today—reviewing parts of sentence—and I'm feeling very pleased with myself. I've budgeted time at the end of class for review, and sure enough my time calculations proved correct. I start our review by keeping it simple:

"All right, let's double check to be sure all these definitions have settled in. I'd like to hear a sentence with a subject, a verb, and a direct object." I pause dramatically, reach into my box of names, and draw out a Popsicle stick identifying Adam.

Adam: "The walrus juggled the marshmallows."

"Excellent! Bravo, Adam. Now, I'd like a sentence with a subject, a verb, a direct object AND an indirect object." Another pause. Another name drawn from the box.

Becky: "The walrus gave the penguin several marshmallows."

"Wonderful. Notice that Becky used a verb that can take an indirect object. Top notch. Now, drum roll please: I'd like a sentence with a subject, a verb, a direct object, an indirect object, AND a prepositional phrase."

With a flourish, I draw Cuthbert's name from the box.

Cuthbert—an affable lad, game for a challenge—looks at me blankly. No response. I move in quickly to fix his distress.

"No worries there Cuthbert. Doing all of that can be quite a challenge. Let's back up to an easier step. Just do what Becky did. Give me a subject, verb, direct and indirect objects."

Cuthbert's expression does not change. I'm not completely sure he's breathing. I keep solving the problem.

"OK. Let's just start with the basics. Just do what Adam did: subject, verb, direct object."

Cuthbert has not blinked in over a minute. He makes no effort to answer my question.

By about this time, I'm starting to feel deep frustration. I can certainly understand why my first question was hard. To assemble a sentence with a subject, a verb, a direct object, an indirect object, and a prepositional phrase does require lots of cognitive juggling. It's understandable that Cuthbert had difficulty doing so. That's why I gave him a somewhat easier task—one that Becky accomplished with ease. And when he couldn't do that, I made the task as easy as it gets: subject, verb, and direct object. Adam rattled off that sentence without even thinking. In fact, now that I think back, Cuthbert raised his hand to offer an example at the beginning of class. Why on earth can't he do so now?

I think Cuthbert just wasn't paying attention. I think he hates my class. I think he hates me! I'm going to give Cuthbert a stern talking to …

Many people, including the teacher in the example above, have a common-sense theory of WM. A student has a certain capacity, and a particular cognitive task either is within that capacity or goes beyond it. For example, creating a sentence with three elements—subject, verb, and direct object—was clearly within Adam's capacity. Becky's WM capacity could manage four elements. And sadly, when this teacher asked for five elements, that task went outside Cuthbert's WM limits. To solve this problem, obviously, the teacher can simply reduce the WM demands: back to four parts of sentence, or even three. If the student can't manage that reduced WM load, well, clearly he's just not trying.

Surprisingly, WM doesn't work this common-sense way. When our students go beyond their WM limits, the entire WM system just might malfunction. Temporarily, at least, their effective WM capacity drops several grades. With an obvious flair for drama, cognitive scientists call this event *catastrophic failure* (Alloway, 2006).

This insight from cognitive science can lead teachers to a terrible realization. It can happen—in fact, it often happens—that our students fail at a WM task because we caused catastrophic failure. The teacher above knows perfectly well that Cuthbert can create this three-element sentence. After all, he offered one up at the beginning of class. But when Cuthbert went beyond his capacity by composing a five-element sentence, his WM temporarily shut down. Asking him to do simpler tasks didn't help because his WM was briefly closed for business.

Of all the insights that teachers gather about WM, this one can be the most painful. Many of us can immediately think of a time that we got angry at a student for failing to do a very simple mental task—only to realize now that we caused that failure to happen. By trying to stretch our students to do their cognitive best, we ended up interrupting their learning.

If you, at this moment, are in the grips of this guilty recognition, go easy on yourself. Many, many teachers have made exactly this mistake. And we did so because no one ever told us what WM is, or how it functions. Now that you know, you can understand your students' cognitive processes much more effectively, and you'll know what to do in the future.

When we first learn about catastrophic failure, teachers often want to know how long it lasts, and how we can repair WM. Since we broke it, we are obviously responsible for fixing it.

Happily, WM will bounce back almost immediately. You yourself have had the experience of feeling cognitively overwhelmed at one moment, and then able to function normally just a few seconds later. When you exit the overstuffed toothpaste aisle in the drugstore, for example, you can choose your shampoo without difficulty. For that reason, this teacher doesn't need to worry about Cuthbert's WM. Instead, he needs to worry about Cuthbert's *emotions*. After all, Cuthbert was just embarrassed in front of his peers, and that embarrassment will last much longer than his WM muddle.

If you see a student fail at a very simple WM task, therefore, ask yourself if that student's WM might have been overloaded just a moment ago. If you conclude that catastrophic failure has happened, you should monitor WM functioning for your other students, and lower cognitive demands if you see them starting to struggle as well.

For Cuthbert, however, you should get to work on restoring your teacherly bond. All teachers have their own ways of doing so. You might make a joke, or apologize, or talk to the student after class. In any case, be sure that Cuthbert has an opportunity to succeed publicly quite soon. Conspicuous success goes a long way toward soothing embarrassment.

This chapter began with two questions. First, as teachers look over upcoming plans, how can we anticipate WM problems? By now, we have some clear answers. WM overload predictably results from

- processing unusually large amounts of new information,
- new combinations of well-known information,
- too much of a good classroom thing (such as instructions, choices, and technology),
- project pedagogies that emphasize teacher-free combining of lots of information, especially by novices, and
- being tired.

Second, we must ask ourselves: If some unanticipated WM overload takes place, how will we know? What will our students do when WM systems begin to stagger? Here again, science shows us several good answers. People under WM duress

- struggle to remember while processing,
- are atypically distractible, and
- experience catastrophic WM failure, so that they can't do perfectly simple cognitive work that they ought to be able to do.

After reading this summary (and figure 2.2), you might feel a bit queasy about your prospects for success. As you can now see, you face a steep WM challenge yourself. You've taken in a lot of new information, and you're trying to combine it with specifics about your own teaching practice. You can feel your end table starting to wobble.

Anticipate WM Overload	Identify WM Overload

1. Too much information:
    new, un/related, combined
2. The Dark Side of the Force:
    instructions, choices, technology
3. Project pedagogies
4. Time of day
	1. Difficulty processing while
	    remembering
	2. Atypical distractibility
	3. Catastrophic failure: surprising
	    difficulty with simple cognitive
	    processes

Solutions to WM Problems	

Figure 2.2   Identifying Working Memory Overload.

Despite your doubts, you also know that learning happens exactly this way. You start by wondering if you'll ever begin to understand a complex topic, and—after the right amount of time and practice—even the nuances of the new field become habit to you. So too with the science of WM. Once you get in the habit of noticing WM demands, of limiting choices, of distinguishing between experts and novices, and of recognizing catastrophic failure, these now-opaque skills will feel like second nature.

And, there is even better news. You don't need to master these concepts fully before you start seeing progress. The first time that you keep your instructions brief and watch your students' cheerful responsiveness, that shot of teacher adrenaline will keep you coming back for more.

The best news is still to come. We've talked for two chapters now about problems. In chapter 3, we finally get to look at solutions.

Chapter Three

Solving Working Memory Problems

At the end of chapter 1, we asked three practical questions about working memory.

1. How can I *anticipate* WM problems?
2. How can I *identify* a WM problem when it occurs?
3. How can I *solve* WM problems? Once I anticipate them (question #1), how do I prevent them from occurring? Once I identify them (question #2), how do I fix them?

Chapter 2 answered the first two questions. We now have several strategies both for anticipating WM overload and for recognizing WM problems that we didn't anticipate. At last, we turn to our third question: How to fix all these problems?

By the way, the Platonic ideal of this book would have followed a somewhat different structure. It would have described one WM problem, and then immediately offered the best solution. This organization, after all, would reduce the WM load for its readers.

Alas, as we will see, WM problems and solutions don't line up so neatly. Instead, many of the solutions described below might work for many of the problems described above. The specific alignment of *this particular problem* with *this particular solution* depends on you. Research can offer several strategies, but only an individual teacher can decide which strategy makes the most sense for these students learning this topic on this day.

COGNITIVE SOLUTIONS TO WORKING MEMORY PROBLEMS

Chapter 3 organizes WM solutions into two groups. The first group helps students manage their thoughts: that is, focuses on *cognitive strategies*. The second group of strategies help manage WM by focusing on students' *emotional* systems.

Strategy #0: Adopt a WM Perspective

When students first enter a new discipline—such as economics—they often start seeing with fresh eyes and fresh insights. Having read an article about sunk costs, for example, an econ neophyte might suddenly see the logic of leaving a dull movie before it is over. In the past, she would have sat through the movie to "get her money's worth," but she can now see through this faulty logic. Even without a professor's prompting, Adam Smith's newest disciple has started to think with an economist's perspective.

At this very moment, you too may be seeing your teaching world from a fresh point of view. If you are an experienced teacher—or even an experienced student—you may now be recalling specific school moments: the time half your students skipped an important step in a lab; the day your best student couldn't answer a basic question; the sure-fire lesson plan that left your class cranky and baffled. As you look back on those puzzling events, they now unveil themselves to you as WM overload.

Equally important, you may already have found solutions to such problems. For example, when experienced teachers hear that long lists of instructions can overwhelm WM, they often suggest a practical solution: write those instructions down. This strategy, as we'll see, typically protects students' WM.

In other words, the foundational solution to WM problems—a strategy so basic that it comes *before* Strategy #1—is to adopt a WM perspective on your teaching. When you remind yourself to notice WM demands, you will automatically recognize pitfalls and problems, as well as strategies and solutions.

The ideas that come to you so naturally may very well have support in the psychology or neuroscience research that we will consider. They might be discussed at length in the pages that follow—but even if they don't and aren't, be sure to keep your ideas in mind. The central argument of this book is not that teachers should follow orders given to us by brain scientists, but that *teachers and researchers should collaborate to help our students learn*. Once you understand the science of WM, your experience will naturally guide you to make practical improvements.

You might pause now, once again, and jot down the ideas that have come to you about helping your students manage WM.

Strategy #1: Solve Working Memory Problems with Long-Term Memory

At the beginning of this book, you undertook a quirky mental challenge: you tried to say your phone number backward. For most people, this cognitive undertaking requires WM—you are, after all, reorganizing information into some new pattern. It's possible, however, that you use your backward phone number as your computer login at work, and so have already memorized those digits in that order. In this case, that mental exercise placed no WM demands on you. You solved a WM problem by using your long-term memory.

The first strategy to solve student WM problems follows this example. If we can support WM processes with knowledge from long-term memory, we can make thinking easier. Teachers have three ways we can use long-term memory stores to bolster WM function.

In the first place, facts that our students already have in long-term memory can make WM processing much easier.

The Sound of Music offers a famous example of this process. When Maria starts teaching her charges to sing, she first rattles off the names of all the notes: do, re, me, fa, sol, and so forth. The children's blank expressions alert her to WM overload. A natural teacher, she goes back to the very beginning and connects each note to an idea already in their long-term memory. "Do," for example, is the name of a female deer. "Mi" sounds like personal pronoun. The result: the children learn to sing, and the rest of us get a fantastic musical number.

A science class might follow Maria's example. When introducing your students to evolution, for instance, you might want them to learn several dates:

- Prokaryotes evolved ~3.6 billion years ago
- Eukaryotes evolved ~2.0 billion years ago
- Amphibians evolved ~360 million years ago
- Mammals evolved ~200 million years ago
- Dinosaurs died out ~65 million years ago
- *Homo sapiens* evolved ~200,000 years ago

The specifics on this list aren't essential, and some of the numbers are controversial. (Eukaryotic life, for example, likely evolved between 1.8 and 2.7 billion years ago.) Your list might include fish or plants. But in any case, it's helpful for students to have some sense of scale, so they can think about evolutionary trajectories of many species.

At the same time, this list creates cognitive problems. Unless your students intern at the Treasury Department, they are unlikely to feel comfortable working with numbers this large. Humans aren't very good at processing high orders of magnitude, and so this list might be more puzzling than helpful.

For example, consider a question that your students might find intriguing: the gap between humans and dinosaurs. Compared to the time that *Homo sapiens* evolved, how long ago did dinosaurs die out? To answer this fun question, we simply need math: we divide 65,000,000 (the time when dinosaurs died out) by 200,000 (the time our species evolved), and—after double-checking on a calculator—we learn that dinosaurs have been dead 325 times longer than *Homo sapiens* have been alive.

That answer is mathematically accurate, and yet oddly unsatisfying. Dinosaurs can thrill, and yet this calculation is frankly rather dull. Can we use our students' long-term memory stores to make this mental processing easier and more meaningful?

The dates above provide information about relative lengths of time. Do students already know some easier system to compare lengths of time? That is, can we support this WM process with knowledge already in long-term memory? Come to think of it, students already know quite an efficient way to make time comparisons: a clock face. The list above quite easily converts into figure 3.1.

Because this clock face organizes information in a way that students instantly recognize—that is, in a way that is well-established in long-term memory—the answer to our dinosaur question could not be clearer. Dinosaurs died out eleven minutes ago; *Homo sapiens* evolved two seconds

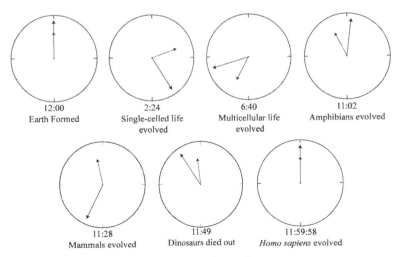

| 12:00 | 2:24 | 6:40 | 11:02 |
| Earth Formed | Single-celled life evolved | Multicellular life evolved | Amphibians evolved |

| 11:28 | 11:49 | 11:59:58 |
| Mammals evolved | Dinosaurs died out | *Homo sapiens* evolved |

Figure 3.1 Evolutionary Peg-Dates Converted Into Time.

ago. The difference between sixty-five million and two hundred thousand is hard to feel; the difference between eleven minutes and two seconds resonates in our bones.

In other words, by connecting new information—the list of evolutionary peg dates—to information that students already have in long-term memory—relative amounts of time as measured on a clock face—we can reduce WM demands to make cognitive processes easier and more meaningful.

To get a head start on the work before you, you might pause now to review the WM problems you identified in chapter 2. As you look over those problems, do you see any that you might fix by drawing on your students' long-term memory stores? Take a minute to emulate Maria's example.

A second approach to converting WM demands into long-term memory work has a thoroughly ugly name: *chunking.* (This technique desperately needs rebranding. It sounds like a fraternity hazing ritual.)

A typical chunking exercise looks like this. During your next department meeting, give half of your colleagues twenty seconds to memorize these letters:

FO XNB CCB SAB CHBO

The other half of the teachers get twenty seconds to memorize these letters:

FOX NBC CBS ABC HBO

You can see, of course, that both groups are memorizing the *same letters in the same order*. And yet, when you test your colleagues 30 minutes later, you will find that the first group remembers relatively few letters, whereas the second group remembers almost all of them.

Teachers in the second group have a relatively simple task. They perceive fifteen letters, but—assuming they know American television networks—they see them in well-known chunks of three. Because those chunks are related to each other, group two can process and remember all fifteen letters quite easily. The first group of teachers, however, faces a steep WM task. If they don't recognize any pattern in those letters, they must try to process and remember all fifteen—a task that goes beyond WM limitations.

The magic of this technique is worth stressing: both groups saw the same letters in the same order. Simply by organizing that information slightly differently, we made a nearly impossible task into a perfectly easy one. In other words, by connecting new information to long-term memory stores, chunking dramatically reduces WM demands.

How can teachers and students use this technique in class? One college student, preparing for an exam on the evolution of human behavior, devised a visual cue to chunk complex material. He drew a rough stick figure of a

person, and its parts prompted him to remember the seven major topics of
the course:

- Mouth → evolution and language
- Arms, sticking out from the torso to resemble a cross → evolution and
  religion
- First hand, reaching out to a few people → evolution and family structure
- Second hand, reaching out to many people → evolution and social structure
- Stomach → evolution and food/nutrition
- Stance, resembling a bathroom icon → evolution and gender roles
- And finally, the crudeness of the stick figure → evolution and art

When writing final exam essays, the student used this mnemonic to ensure
his answers were complete. By mentally working his way down the stick
figure, he made sure that each essay covered all seven course topics. Without
this chunking shortcut, he would have relied on WM to keep track of the topics he had covered and those left to discuss: a WM demand that would have
made planning his essays noticeably more difficult. A simple stick figure in
long-term memory thus promoted WM functioning.

Each teacher will use chunking differently. If you teach elementary school,
you know that funny songs can be powerful mnemonics; they help students
chunk information. For older students, too cool for such games, acronyms
might do the trick. You might provide your students with a chunking system,
or you might make it their homework to devise one on their own. You might
swap chunking ideas with your colleagues to expand your repertoire.

Helpful neuroscience research done by Daniel Bor's team (Bor, Cumming,
Scott, & Owen, 2004; Bor, Duncan, Wiseman, & Owen, 2003) gives teachers
extra confidence that chunking can help students learn. In these studies, Bor's
participants lay in an functional magnetic resonance imaging (fMRI) scanner.
At times they heard and repeated readily chunkable information. In the 2004
study, for example, they heard a set of digits with a clear pattern: 9-7-5-3-2-
4-6-8. At other times, they heard and repeated a random set of digits: 9-2-6-
5-3-8-7-1. Bor's team found that brains consistently involve more prefrontal
regions in the processing of readily chunkable information.

It's easy to over-interpret Bor's data. We might be tempted to say that Bor's
research reveals the "chunking part of the brain." However, we must keep in
mind that all complex cognitive processes happen in widely diffuse neural
networks. No one part of the brain is solely responsible for any intricate
thought patterns. We might also be tempted to say that "because more areas
of the brain are involved in chunking, we know that students are doing more
thinking." While that interpretation sounds plausible, we should remember
that additional neural activation does not always benefit cognition. Fluent
readers, for example, use less brain real estate than dyslexic readers.

Instead, Bor's research helps teachers by giving us an extra reason to be confident. Based on our own classroom experience, we have good reason to believe that chunking is an effective strategy. Chunks in long-term memory seem to reduce WM processing demands. If that's true, we should expect that brains process easy-to-chunk information differently than they process hard-to-chunk information. Bor's studies confirm that prediction. Happily, neuroscience supports our classroom experience.

Teachers can shift WM load to long-term memory by explicitly connecting new ideas to our students' current knowledge, and by deliberately chunking new information. We can also build well-established routines to transform WM tasks into long-term memory knowledge.

In your class, you might insist that every homework assignment have the same heading: name on the top right, date on the top left, and title of the assignment in the center. When second graders get ready to go to the lunch room, you might have them practice several specific steps: stand up, push the desk chair in, return supplies to cubbies, and line up at the door. When seniors write bibliographies for their research papers, they must follow the very precise requirements of the APA style sheet: last name, first initial, date in parentheses, and journal title in italics with only the first word capitalized.

The first time that your students follow these instructions, they have to manipulate each one in WM. The longer the instruction list, the more taxing the WM demand. However, if you ensure that this list of instructions never varies, it becomes a routine: part of their long-term memory store. Relatively quickly, the WM demand of these tasks falls to zero. Once you sense that a routine has been internalized, you can add new WM demands on top of it. Students might turn in extra worksheets on their way to the lunch line, or cite a source with multiple authors in their bibliography. Because the underlying process is well established in long-term memory, this extra step—which might have overwhelmed WM a few weeks ago—goes without a hitch.

Cognitive routines, like procedural routines, reduce WM demands. When students memorize the multiplication table, learn sight words, or commit lines to heart, they free up cognitive resources to solve complex math problems, read chapter books, or ponder their character's motivations (Willingham, 2009). Memorization isn't sexy, and is often belittled with adjectives like "mere" or "rote." And yet, if students memorize essentials, that knowledge reduces WM demands.

What should students memorize? Any information or definition or process that they will use routinely in more advanced work. You may get pushback from your students and even your colleagues. But your students will thank you when their long-term memory stores free up WM capacity later in the year.

In sum, to solve the WM problems that we anticipate and identify, we can start by relying on long-term memory. By connecting new information to knowledge already in long-term memory, by chunking material, and by creating routines, we reduce WM demands and make learning easier.

A final note on this strategy: we must acknowledge one key long-term memory danger—our own. We already know the material we are teaching, and our intuitive understanding can blind us to our students' WM burden. As noted above, a biology teacher might underestimate the difficulty of connecting the respiratory, circulatory, and urinary systems because she already understands those connections so well. As we think about using long-term memory to reduce students' WM stresses, we should remind ourselves that they are just starting to learn what we already know very well.

Strategy #2: Redistribute Working Memory Demands

In chapter 2, an eager intern suggested a lesson plan for your "20th Century American History through Music" class: you could introduce a term's worth of musical vocabulary on the first day. As an experienced teacher, you could see right away that this plan would flood your students' WM. And yet, as you contemplated solutions, you saw no obvious way to solve that problem with the first WM strategy. You could not rely on prior knowledge, or chunk the material, or create useful routines. Strategy #1 helps with some WM problems, but not with this one.

A second strategy can reduce WM difficulties, specifically when students face information overload. Rather than give them lots of information at once, we can spread it out over time. In brief, we can *redistribute* WM demands to ensure they don't all come on top of each other.

In the case of this history class, you can redistribute musical terminology quite easily. Rather than introduce all the terms in the first class, bring them up as needed. Students can learn about "syncopation" and "scat" in the 1920s, but you can hold off on "whammy bar" until later in the course. If you have to cover three new theorems in today's geometry class, you might introduce a new one every fifteen minutes, rather than presenting all three right at the beginning. If a short story in Spanish has several new vocabulary words, you might space them out in blocks of five rather than define them all at once.

This strategy, in fact, has probably occurred to you already; you might think of it as part of Strategy #0. Once you learned about WM limitations, you immediately saw that an overlarge WM load could easily be subdivided into perfectly manageable parts.

At the same time, this approach does include some subtleties. The first, rules and exceptions. Rules reduce WM load, but exceptions increase them.

If I were a French teacher, for example, I might alert my students to this helpful rule: "all French nouns ending in -ette are feminine." This rule provides my students with substantial WM relief. Because English does not gender nouns, native speakers of English struggle to understand why—much less remember that—a chair is feminine and couch is masculine. While creating new sentences, they must rapidly adjust pronouns and adjectives to agree with those mysterious genders—a strenuous WM challenge. By giving them a rule that simplifies this load even slightly, by letting them know that "all French nouns ending in -ette are feminine," I reduce that challenge in a most helpful way. In effect, rules chunk information and thereby reduce cognitive demands.

Because I want to be thorough and precise, I decide to tell my students the complete rule: "all French nouns ending in -ette are feminine, except for *squelette*."

This version has the benefits of accuracy. However, it commits the grave teaching offense of needlessly raising WM load. With this version, students have to remember that there is a rule about -ette nouns, they have to remember what that rule is, they have to remember that there are exceptions, and they have to remember what the exception is. And, Halloween isn't widely celebrated in France, so it's not obvious that they'll be using the French word for "skeleton" any time soon.

Teachers who understand the role of WM in learning follow this principle: provide rules, and save exceptions for later.

Is it true that, according to the rules of English grammar, the subject of a verb is *never* in a prepositional phrase? Well, it's true enough. Once your students have mastered that rule, you can tell them about words like "most," "half," and "some," where they must look into a prepositional phrase to determine if the subject is singular or plural. ("Half of the apple is on the table." "Half of the apples are on the table.")

Is it true that, after 1440, *all* of the Holy Roman Emperors were Habsburgs? It's true enough. If students read about the three-year reign of Charles VII, you can tell them about the exception. (It's probable that Charles VII's mother is the only person who cares very much.)

Is it true that generals should *always* consolidate their forces before attacking an enemy? It's true enough. If you discuss Robert E. Lee, you can explore his repeated defiance of this maxim.

Of course, our students enjoy catching us making mistakes, and so we must be careful in introducing these exceptions. When you tell your students that the solid form of a substance is *always* denser than its liquid form, you might also alert them that an important exception will show up in next week's reading. But if they don't need that information right now—and they're not going ice-fishing this weekend—then you can let them master the rule before you complicate it with the bizarre properties of water.

In brief, by leading with rules and redistributing exceptions to later in the syllabus, we can simplify WM demands.

This redistribution strategy helps in a third way as well. If a particular homework assignment places an unusually high demand on WM, you might redistribute that challenge by having students get started on it during class. Once they've processed the potentially overwhelming parts with your assistance, they can manage a more typical workload at home. (Because WM varies with time of day, you might also encourage them to tackle the hardest part of the homework earlier rather than later in the evening.)

To sum up, when a particular lesson plan dumps too much information all at once, teachers can spread that information across the class or across several days. We should pay particular attention to rules and exceptions, and to homework assignments with unusually high WM demands.

Note that these three approaches redistribute WM burdens *over time*. We should also be careful to redistribute those burdens *across modality*. A study by Mayer, Bove, Bryman, Mars, and Tapangco (1996) helps us see the remarkable benefits of this strategy.

Mayer's team asked three groups of students to learn about lightning. Group A read a 600-word passage explaining how lightning forms, and then took a quiz on that passage. This quiz required them to use the information they read in a new way. For instance, they were asked what they might do to decrease the intensity of lightning during a storm—a question not explicitly discussed in the passage. Because the students had to reorganize the information they read into a new answer, this test placed high-WM demands on them. Group A solved, on average, 2.3 problems.

In some way, this result is good news. For several centuries, Western education has asked students to read information and then solve new problems based on that reading. The students in Group A had some success in this process, so it's good to know that students can do what we've been asking them to do all along.

Mayer then gave Group B the same passage. However, that passage was accompanied by five diagrams highlighting the various stages of lightning formation.

Next, Group C studied the five diagrams that Group B saw, but they did not read the passage. (All three groups, by the way, got the same amount of time to learn about lightning.) How did these Groups B and C do on Mayer's test?

You can see the remarkable results in figure 3.2. Group B—which saw the diagrams and the passage—scored a 4.9. Group C—which saw the diagrams but not the passage—scored a 4.6. In other words, students who saw the diagrams at least doubled the score of the students who did not.

Mayer's study highlights an essential point: teachers can redistribute WM demands from words to visuals. When students use both verbal and visual systems to manage WM tasks—such as applying new information about lightning to new questions—they are dramatically more successful.

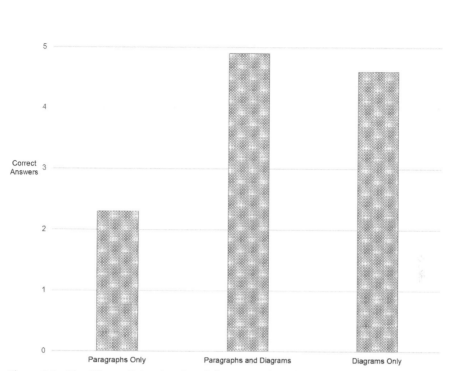

Figure 3.2   The Effect of Visual and Verbal Presentation of Information about Lightning on Working Memory and Learning. *Source*: **Based on Mayer et al. (1996).**

A similar study focusing on geometry learning points to the same conclusion (Mousavi, Low, & Sweller, 1995). In this study, high-school students studied new theorems. Half of these students looked at a diagram of a geometry problem and read the steps leading to a solution. These students took in all their information visually. A second group looked at the same diagram and listened to an audiotape of those same solution steps. This second group of students got exactly the same information, but divided the WM load between visual and verbal channels.

To see which group learned the material better, Mousavi then gave both groups new geometry problems. Crucially, he measured how long it took for students to find the right answers. He found that students who got all their information visually took as much as 50 percent longer than those who got information visually and verbally. By redistributing WM demands to both visual and verbal channels, Mousavi increased students' WM success.

This redistribution strategy helps explain many of the strategies that come so intuitively to teachers. Once we understand how instructions tax WM, for example, most of us quickly see the benefits of writing them down. Of course, writing instructions down makes them visual. So, too, the clock-face strategy described above, where the science teacher presented evolutionary peg dates in a more familiar form. That approach lowers WM demands both by connecting new information to prior knowledge (Strategy #1) and by shifting WM demands to the visual channel (Strategy #2).

Thus, when you anticipate a WM hot spot or identify WM crunch during class, you might search for ways to create a visual representation of the required thought processes. Can you write something on the board? Is there a photograph, a chart, a diagram, or a graphic organizer that presents their cognitive work more handily? Or, if the information is already visual, can you supplement it with verbal support?

For example, in chapter 2, Cuthbert experienced catastrophic failure when the teacher asked him to compose a sentence with five grammatical elements. Cuthbert faced steep WM demands, *all of which were verbal*. If the teacher had predicted this WM collapse, he might have prevented it by writing earlier sentences on the board. Becky, for example, had already provided four of the grammatical elements: "The walrus gave the penguin several marshmallows." If that sentence were visible on the board, Cuthbert could use both visual and verbal channels to add a prepositional phrase: "The walrus gave the penguin several marshmallows *after high tea*."

One strategy for making information visual seems especially handy: students can take notes.

This particular approach, at first glance, has much to recommend it. Because students must think harder when they take notes, it seems likely that they will learn more. As will be discussed in book three of this series, appropriate cognitive effort yields long-term knowledge. Presumably, the students' own notes are especially beneficial for restudy, because students take notes that align most efficiently with their own thinking.

And yet, the benefits of note taking may come at a substantial WM cost (Kellogg, 2001; Olive, Kellogg, & Piolat, 2008). In many classrooms, students take notes while the teacher is speaking. In order to do so, the student must process the ideas being explained by the teacher (WM challenge #1), decide which ones to write down (challenge #2), reword those ideas into phrases short enough to jot down quickly (challenge #3), engage in the manual and visuo-spatial work of writing (challenges #4+5)—all while processing and evaluating what the teacher is currently saying (challenges #6+7). Any pair of these demands might muddle WM; all seven of them are likely to crush it.

At those times when we want our students to take notes, we must therefore be scrupulous about minimizing the conflict among these demands. The goal is clear: *we should never ask our students to write down new, complex ideas at the same time that we explain them.*

We might, for example, divide the process into distinct phases. First, with their pencils on their desks, our students listen to us define *inelastic demand*, or outline the Great Compromise of 1787, or explain the use of the passé composé. Second, they replay those ideas in their heads, think about the most important elements, and perhaps confer with their classmates. Third, they write down the essentials. During this second step, we say nothing—or, perhaps, answer clarifying questions. During the third step, we continue to say nothing—but circle the room looking at what our students have written. In this way, we ensure they don't have to listen, prioritize, understand, and write all at the same time.

In another strategy, we might give students a substantial outline with essential words blanked out. In this model, students fill in key words as we speak. This approach has several benefits. It substantially reduces WM load, because the student has a well-organized record of all the important ideas. Students need not prioritize, reword, or organize new concepts. Being less time consuming than the pencils-down strategy above, it allows us to cover much more content.

At the same time, this approach reduces the amount of healthy cognitive work that the students must do. In other words, by providing a WM solution, it may create a long-term memory problem. We might opt for this strategy to make initial learning more productive, but we must be sure to provide extra cognitive challenges later during the learning process to solidify long-term memories.

If the ideas under discussion aren't new or all that complex, then students might very well be able to take concurrent notes. After all, they've got long-term memory supporting this process. If, however, the ideas are new and complex, we must deliberately rethink note taking as a classroom task. Your experience and your colleagues will guide you in discovering the best way to prevent WM overload.

In sum, we can redistribute WM demands in time by spreading out WM load, by leading with rules and saving exceptions for later, and by starting WM-intensive homework in class. We can redistribute WM demands across modalities by ensuring that cognitive work is both visual and verbal—as long as visual presentation doesn't require students to take concurrent notes on new, complex information.

Strategy #3: Reduce Working Memory Demands

Looking over tomorrow's lesson plan, you abruptly realize that the quiz on the passive periphrastic might well demand too much of your sixth graders' WM. You don't have an intuition about solving the problem (Strategy #0), and you don't see any way to rely on their long-term memory banks (Strategy #1). After much head-scratching, you can't see how to redistribute those demands over time or across modality (Strategy #2). And yet you do not blanch, because you've always got Strategy #3: reduce WM demands. If students face too steep a WM climb, lower its grade.

The challenge of this strategy, of course, lies in finding the right balance: How to reduce WM demands without reducing learning? When is an exercise simple enough without being oversimplified? To solve this problem, teachers should look for parts of the WM load that don't contribute directly to the immediate learning goal.

Tracy and Ross Alloway (2015) give a helpful example of enhancing learning by reducing WM demands. They observed a class in which students were practicing the concepts *first, third,* and *last.* To help her charges along, the teacher asked her students to color in the first, third, and last flower in a row. When there were ten flowers on the page, some students found the task overwhelming and began coloring them in randomly.

The teacher quickly realized that the large number of flowers overwhelmed the students' WM. Of course, there was no particular reason to have ten flowers; that number didn't contribute to the lesson's goal. She solved the problem quite easily by reducing the number of flowers to five. This change lowered the WM load of the task while still allowing enough of a cognitive challenge to promote learning. The next week, these same students were able to learn *second, fourth,* and *fifth* quite easily. In this case, the total number of flowers wasn't relevant to the learning objective. By reducing that part of the WM load, the teacher wisely focused on the goal of the lesson: learning ordinal numbers.

A high-school English teacher, recalling that his students' first batch of essays were a disorganized muddle, might decide to focus the next set narrowly on effective structure. Given this focus, he might give his students two or three potential thesis statements and dedicate each night's homework specifically to organizational goals. The first night, students compose topic sentences and discuss the best order for those three arguments. The second night, they gather supporting evidence for each topic sentence and ponder the most effective arrangement of those examples. The final night—having already done the organizational planning—they compose the essay.

In this assignment, the teacher has deliberately removed other kinds of cognitive effort from the rubric. He is not (at this point) looking for original argumentation. He is not (at this point) looking for subordinated quotations or logical parallelism or strong verbs. He is not (at this point) looking for connections to other works of literature or to current events. By narrowing the goals of the assignment specifically to structure, he allows his students to devote all their WM resources to this one essential skill. Once they have made progress in organizing their essays—and, given the format of the assignment, they are likely to do so—his students can use their WM to make more sophisticated arguments, or to write more elegant prose, on the following assignment.

The Latin teacher above who worried about her quiz might recognize its competing WM demands. First, this quiz asks students to form the passive periphrastic by combining the gerundive with the appropriate form of "sum." Second, the quiz gives students the chance to practice new vocabulary.

Although students need to master both verbs forms and vocabulary to improve their Latin, they might not be able to handle both simultaneously. After some thought, the teacher concludes that—at this moment on the syllabus—the verb conjugation outranks the vocabulary practice. For this reason, she decides to include a word bank on the quiz. By reducing the WM demands of processing new words, this strategy ensures that students have enough cognitive bandwidth to insist that *Carthago delenda est.*

The Alloways also have specific advice about reducing instructions. In their analysis, 5- to 6-year-olds can typically process 2 instructions; 7- to 9-year-olds, 3 instructions; 10- to 12-year-olds, 4 instructions; 13- to 15-year-olds, 5 instructions; and 16- to 29-year-olds, 6 instructions. (Alloway, T., & Alloway, R., 2015). If you predict a WM overload, try reducing the number of instructions to fit within these limits. Of course, these numbers should not be taken as absolutes, but as helpful starting points. If you give your fifth graders four instructions and they can't manage that number, you should simply step back to three. In fact, if the instructions require lots of movement or lots of supplies, you might find it helpful to give one instruction and wait until all students have completed it before giving the next.

This strategy requires patience. Knowing how much material we have to cover, we can often find ourselves rushing to get more material into each class, each week, and each assignment. Yet, now that we know how WM limitations affect learning, we know that incremental progress builds long-term memory stores. These cognitive assets will help with more advanced work later on— even though WM capacity has remained exactly the same (figure 3.3).

Anticipate WM Overload	Identify WM Overload
1. Too much information: new, un/related, combined 2. The Dark Side of the Force: instructions, choices, technology 3. Project pedagogies 4. Time of day	1. Difficulty processing while remembering 2. Atypical distractibility 3. Catastrophic failure: surprising difficulty with simple cognitive processes
Solutions to WM Problems	

Cognitive Solutions
 Strategy #0: Adopt a WM perspective
 Strategy #1: Use long-term memory to support WM processing
 Strategy #2: Redistribute WM demands...
     ...over time
     ...across visual and verbal modalities
 Strategy #3: Reduce WM demands, wisely	

Figure 3.3 Cognitive Solutions to Working Memory Problems.

EMOTIONAL SOLUTIONS TO WORKING MEMORY PROBLEMS

Strategies #0–3 focus on cognitive approaches to reducing WM problems. By shifting mental work into long-term memory, by redistributing WM demands, and by reducing them, we can make thinking easier and more effective.

At the same time, teachers know that thinking does not happen in a vacuum. Our students' cognitive systems interact with most other brain processes, and so their emotional state matters to learning. When we keep both sets of solutions in mind, we are likelier to help WM processing for all our students.

Strategy #4: Normalize Struggle

Students often labor under a strange misconception. They believe that smart people learn without working very hard. This foolish belief has a dark side: if students do have to work hard in school, they might believe that they are not smart.

French researchers Autin and Croizet (2012) wondered if they could help students out of this demoralizing thought pattern. In particular, they wanted to help students perceive difficulty as a normal part of learning, rather than a sign of ignorance. To test their hypothesis, they asked a group of sixth graders to solve very difficult anagram puzzles.

The researchers told half the sixth graders that they wanted to study the strategies that students used to solve anagrams. This group, in other words, thought of their cognitive struggle as part of the researchers' work. By contrast, they guided the second group to see struggle as a normal part of learning. Autin and Croizet used a bike riding analogy to make their point:

> Do you remember when you did not know how to ride a bike? Was it easy or difficult to ride the first time? Yes, it was difficult and it is *normal that children find it difficult* precisely because they have not yet learned how to do it. Well it is the same thing for these [anagram] exercises. When you're in a situation like you are in right now, what you need to do is to practice, to learn little by little how to solve them. While practicing *you'll keep trying things that do not work out, but it's fine* because that is actually how you learn. You cannot get it right immediately. (Autin & Croizet, 2012, p. 9, emphasis added)

This passage emphasizes that struggle is a normal part of learning; hence, the technique is called *normalizing struggle*. No one learns to ride a bike the first time; no one learns *anything* the first time. All people, including smart people, struggle to learn.

How did this pep talk affect the sixth graders' performance on a subsequent WM test? On the easy WM questions, it didn't make much difference. But as the test got more and more difficult, the pep talk increasingly helped. At the second highest level of difficulty, for example, the students who heard that struggle is normal scored roughly 65 percent; those who did not scored below 50 percent.

The effectiveness of Autin and Croizet's technique merits some exploration. In chapter 1, we saw that WM capacity cannot be artificially increased. Yet here, in under ten minutes, Autin and Croizet's pep talk boosted WM function. How can this be?

Autin and Croizet's theory is not that they have increased WM capacity, but that they have increased the students' ability to use the WM capacity they have. The students who didn't get the pep talk presumably used some of their WM to dwell on negative self-talk. "I'm really struggling at these exercises," they said to themselves. "I guess I'm just not the kind of person who is good at these things. Why am I even trying?"

The students who did get the pep talk, however, pivoted quickly away from such thoughts. "I'm really struggling at these exercises," they thought. "But ... wait ... struggle is normal—like when I learned to ride a bike. So, I'm just going to keep at it." Both groups had the same WM capacity, but the normalize struggle group used that capacity more effectively. By changing the students' perception of difficulty, this technique helped them use their cognitive powers to the fullest.

Of course, teachers have helped students perceive struggle as normal for as long as teaching has existed. Doubtless, you already have your own times and methods to do so. Psychology research suggests four ways to hone our technique.

First, we should normalize struggle before assignments that have a high-WM load. Autin and Croizet's research suggests that the technique frees up WM capacity, and so it can be especially beneficial at times when we can predict WM challenges.

Second, this technique adds a helpful agenda item to your next department or grade-level meeting. When you meet with your trigonometry colleagues, you might ask them: What topics from the upcoming unit do our students find most challenging? Once you have gathered this information, you can normalize struggle all the more persuasively. If you learn that everyone's students had difficulty understanding Euler's formula last year, you can reassure this year's crew that their puzzlement is typical. Over time, they will—like generations of students before them—understand these concepts quite clearly.

Third, the technique is especially effective when students make it personal. In a study by Walton and Cohen (2011), for example, college freshmen read about the struggles that seniors at their college had experienced during their first year. When those freshmen then contemplated how their own struggles matched those of the seniors, they saw a remarkable improvement in their grades over four years of college. Because these students both understood struggle to be normal and explicitly linked their own experience to that message, they internalized the lesson more meaningfully.

This third technique suggests a *fourth*: give students the chance to talk with each other about the difficulties they have experienced. Students are especially likely to believe that struggle is normal if they hear directly from their peers. Claude Steele (2011) found that late-night small group "bull sessions" (Steele, 2011, p. 166) were particularly helpful in convincing students that everyone struggles to learn. In other words, we can tell our students that difficulties are typical, and we can let them tell each other.

If you are familiar with Carol Dweck's work on *mindset* or Claude Steele's research into *stereotype threat*, you doubtless recognize normalizing struggle as a technique that they research and advocate. (The second book of this series explores these connections more fully.) For the time being, we should all remember Autin and Croizet's research: normalizing struggle improves our students' WM processes. The cognitive struggles we anticipated and identified in chapter 2 might be prevented with this well-researched technique.

Strategy #5: Reduce Pressure

Our final strategy for fixing WM problems starts with an ethical problem and includes rather comical solutions.

Sian Beilock and Thomas Carr wanted to investigate the effects of pressure on WM function. This question poses a thorny problem: how can researchers ethically pressure study participants? Presumably they can't tie them to the track of an onrushing train. Relying, no doubt, on a wicked sense of humor, here's what they did:

Students came to Beilock and Carr's lab to take a math test (2005). After they completed the first half of the test, those students learned that they would receive a cash bonus if their score went up by 10 percent on the second half of the test. (Pressure #1: cash incentive.)

And then the researchers updated this story slightly. Each student learned that, in fact, she had been anonymously paired with another student. Only if *both* students in the pair raised their scores by 10 percent would both get the prize. If either one fell short, then they both lost out. And, when Beilock and Carr "checked their records," they saw that this student's (imaginary) partner had already taken the test. Sure enough, her score had gone up by 10 percent. So, now the student's own cash reward *and her partner's cash reward* depended on the upcoming test. (Pressure #2: peer/group pressure.)

And by the way, this poor student then heard that math teachers and professors wanted to study the strategies that students use to solve these math problems. For this reason, Beilock and Carr said that they would videotape the students as they worked on the second half of the test, and this footage would be examined to learn more about effective and ineffective strategies. (Pressure #3: observation pressure.)

Beilock and Carr used these diabolical instructions on two groups of students: those with relatively high-WM capacity and those with a relatively low-WM capacity.

When they looked at all these variables, what did they find on the second half of the math test?

First, pressure made no difference when participants solved *easy math problems*. With or without pressure, both high-WM-capacity and low-WM-capacity students did equally well. When the work wasn't challenging, in other words, students didn't need much WM capacity to solve the problems. All that pressure didn't interfere with their ability to do so.

However, when these students solved *hard math problems*, the pattern changed—and changed in surprising ways. When the low-WM-capacity students solved difficult problems, their scores remained about the same after pressure. In fact, although the difference was not statistically significant, their scores got slightly better. (Why would their scores improve? Well, perhaps, the practice they got on the first half of the test helped them do well on the second half.)

Unlike the low-WM-capacity students, the high-WM-capacity students saw their scores fall roughly 10 percent. On the first half of the test, before the pressure, they scored dramatically higher than the low-WM-capacity students. On the second half of the test, after the pressure, their scores were about the same as those low-WM-capacity students.

In brief, pressure converts a high-WM-capacity student into a low-WM-capacity student. Pressure, that is, can reduce WM.

Having studied Beilock and Carr's research, teachers should doubtless contemplate ways to reduce some of the pressures that our students face. In particular, we should be interested in the three kinds of pressure that these researchers applied. Although teachers rarely use cash incentives (Pressure #1), grades might feel like cash incentives to our students. Depending on our teaching habits, group projects might have students rely on each for grades (Pressure #2). Likewise, our supervision of students might at times make them feel like we're videotaping them (Pressure #3).

If these pressures coincide with a WM overload, we might solve that problem by reducing pressure. We might, for example, reduce *grade pressure* by marking quizzes pass/fail. We might reduce *group pressure* by reevaluating our group-project rubric. We might reduce *supervision pressure* by giving students more space to work on their own. The best strategy will depend on the specific circumstances of your classroom and your students. But we can help students who face WM difficulties by keeping these options in mind.

Of course, Beilock and Carr's research should not persuade us to remove all pressures from school. Even if we could accomplish such a goal, that success would do our students little good. To be successful adults, and to be successful teachers, we need to be able to manage pressure. One way we learn to do that is by *practicing*, both at home and at school. Students will learn how to manage pressure well only if they have the chance to face the right-sized challenge at the right time.

In other words, we should not set about to eliminate all school pressures. Instead, at moments of WM overload, we should be on the lookout for any relevant pressure. If we identify such a stressor, we might perfectly well conclude that—at this particular moment—a student will benefit more from toughing her way through a difficult situation. In this case, we would keep the pressure levels where they are, even if that level means the student doesn't succeed at the WM task. However, if we decide that the cognitive success takes precedence over this momentary opportunity for emotional growth, then we can reduce pressure enough to allow for cognitive success.

This kind of in-the-moment balancing act can never be scripted. Few absolute rules govern these decisions, and many wise teachers might argue for different choices at any one moment. However, we will make these decisions more wisely when we recognize both the importance of WM function and the ways that pressure can hamper its success.

Figure 3.4 summarizes all the strategies discussed in the chapter. When chapter 2 alerts us to potential WM problems, we can follow the research-aligned strategies of chapter 3. Long-term memory can support WM processes, and thereby reduce cognitive struggle. Teachers can redistribute WM demands over time or across modalities; we can also reduce WM demands by focusing precisely on learning goals. Recognizing the importance of our students' emotional lives, we can also normalize struggle and reduce the pressures of the classroom.

By the way, figure 3.4 also enacts some of the advice it contains. In particular, by reorganizing the ideas of part I into a visual form, it divides the WM load of the book between words and pictures. And, by gradually building this

Anticipate WM Overload	Identify WM Overload
1. Too much information: new, un/related, combined 2. The Dark Side of the Force: instructions, choices, technology 3. Project pedagogies 4. Time of day	1. Difficulty processing while remembering 2. Atypical distractibility 3. Catastrophic failure: surprising difficulty with simple cognitive processes
Solutions to WM Problems	

Cognitive Solutions
Strategy #0: Adopt a WM perspective
Strategy #1: Use long-term memory to support WM processing
Strategy #2: Redistribute WM demands...
          ...over time
          ...across visual and verbal modalities
Strategy #3: Reduce WM demands, wisely

Emotion Solutions
Strategy #4: Normalize struggle
Strategy #5: Manage pressure

Figure 3.4   Emotional Solutions to Working Memory Problems.

diagram up over several dozen pages, part I has eased this summary into your long-term memory banks. Given the WM complexity of the material you've covered, you deserve all the cognitive relief you can get.

Chapter 4 briskly summarizes part I, gives an extended example of these techniques from an ecology class, and then answers several frequently asked questions.

Chapter Four

Working Memory Review with FAQ

The first three chapters have covered a lot of ground. Ironically, you have had to absorb so much new information about working memory that your own working memory may have been overloaded at times. For this reason, it's worthwhile to pause and go over the major ideas of part I.

To learn almost anything, students must combine new information with their prior knowledge. Just as you reorganize old photographs into a memorable new album, your students use their WM to sort and reshuffle ideas, processes, facts, and skills. If you've got a small table on which to manage your photos, you need to think carefully about using its narrow confines effectively. So too, our students need help managing their limited WM resources. Since we can't (yet) increase WM capacity, we must become experts at working within the capacity they have.

Like all kinds of expertise, WM expertise will take time, practice, energy, and determination. And, without a doubt, it will improve your teaching and help your students learn more.

The first step, learn to spot WM problems before they arise. We know that too much new information can overload WM, especially if the new facts or ideas aren't obviously related to one another. Equally problematic, new combinations of information—sometimes called "critical thinking," sometimes called "creativity"—place very high demands on cognitive functioning.

Just as the Force has both a Light and a Dark Side, so too several otherwise beneficial teaching practices can flood WM. Instructions can help students, but too many instructions can take over their end tables. So too with choices and many kinds of technology. Some project pedagogies encourage large amounts of information and lots of choices and thus might be too much for beginners. And, as a practical matter, WM capacity can fluctuate during the day.

Knowing these potential dangers, we can review our teaching plans—lessons, tests, and syllabi—to root them out.

The second expertise step: recognizing a student's behavior as a WM problem. (Because they can't tell us that their WM is hurting, we have to figure out this problem on our own.) A student who can't keep track of a large pool of information while processing one part of it has probably run out of WM space. Although all students are occasionally distractible, *atypical* distractibility suggests WM problems. And when a student can't do a very simple cognitive process—can't even offer up a subject, verb, and direct object— this catastrophic failure of WM lets us know that we've been asking for too much. With this expert knowledge, we can diagnose a WM struggle and fix the problem on the fly.

Finally, WM experts know how to manage all these problems. In some cases, our teacherly instincts kick in: the problem, once recognized, suggests its own solution. If not, we can start by drawing on our students' long-term memory. We might align new ideas with familiar ones. We might—despite the dreadful name—chunk information. We might deliberately build up consistent routines.

If long-term memory offers no relief, we might redistribute WM demands. We can spread information out over time, especially by leading with rules and postponing exceptions. We can also move atypical WM challenges out of the homework and into the classroom. In a pinch, we can reduce WM demands. By focusing precisely on each lesson's goal, we can eliminate extraneous WM demands.

Teachers can enhance these cognitive strategies by attending to our students' emotional lives. When we remind our students that struggle is normal, they spend less time worrying about their own difficulties and more time thinking about their work. In other words, they use less WM capacity for negative self-talk, and more for cognitive performance. Likewise, we know that pressure can impede WM function, especially for our stronger students. Students, of course, need practice at managing pressure, and so schools should allow them the opportunity to struggle and to fail. At times, however, WM success may be more important than a broader lesson about handling pressure. At such times, we might reduce an emphasis on grades, or on group work, or careful supervision.

Expertise would be easier to come by if the WM problems identified in the first two steps neatly aligned with solutions in the third. In reality, they simply don't. For this reason, individual teachers must use our experience and our wisdom to link problems with solutions. A music teacher might use prior knowledge to help students learn the names of all the notes. A biology teacher might use visuals to help students see how the lungs connect to the kidneys. A calculus teacher might start homework in class when her students first try to find the area under a two-hump curve. In each case, their students will learn more.

A SAMPLE LESSON PLAN REVIEW

As this brief summary shows, we strive not only to learn information about WM, but also to learn how to think about WM. This fresh thought process might go something like this.

Next week, your ecology class will be studying *trophic cascade*—one of your favorite topics in the course. The concept itself is simple enough: a change at the top of a food chain leads to dramatic developments throughout the environment. You will use the classic example of wolves in Yellowstone National Park.

When wolves were reintroduced in 1995, they hunted the deer away from the open plains by the rivers. These altered grazing patterns meant that new grasses, shrubs, and even trees could grow without being eaten away by the deer. This new habitat allowed birds to flourish, and provided raw material for beavers to build dams—dams that created more new habitats for other species as well. The wolves also reduced the population of the coyotes, and their reduction led to an increase in small rodent populations. More rodents, more rodent predators: foxes, weasels, and bald eagles.

You particularly like this unit because it includes one of your favorite tests. In past years, you have asked your students to speculate what would happen in another environment if a new top predator were introduced. Students might-write about the Cloud Forest in Costa Rica, or the Amazon River, or the South Shetland Islands, or another environment of their choosing. Although it seemed daunting, this test question allowed students both to review what they already know about those environments—which you had studied in earlier units—and to see fresh connections among many species within any one ecosystem.

You decide to review this unit with WM limitations in mind, and so you take out your syllabus, lesson plans, and test from last year. As you begin looking them over, you recall a sad discrepancy: although trophic cascade is one of your favorite topics, your students never seem to get into it as much as you thought they would. Perhaps your WM perspective will explain this troubling pattern.

Your first question: can you *anticipate* any parts of the unit that might overload WM?

Well, to start with, the Yellowstone example does include all sorts of *new information*. The case study includes about twenty species, and you often discussed several others as well. Because you wanted students to develop the habit of thinking like biologists, you have asked them to learn scientific names for the species (wolf, for example, is *Canis lupus*), and that requirement added substantially to their processing burden. Truthfully, much of this new information is also *unrelated*, or at least not obviously related. As someone who loves trees, you see right away why cottonwoods and aspens would move in after the deer departed. But students who don't know that these species typically follow shrubs will think of them as two distinct species, not as members of a functional group.

At the same time, the lesson requires students to *combine* all of this new and unrelated information. They need to trace the connection from wolf to deer to aspen to beaver to otter, and from wolf to coyote to mountain vole to raven. Really? Mountain vole (*Microtus montanus*)?

Does this unit require *creativity*? Indeed, the test asks students to imagine how a new predator would influence all the species below it in the food chain. And, as a particular creativity challenge, students then need to envision the effects throughout the food chain for each of those subsequent changes. For example, the wolf's reduction of coyotes increases rodents, and also the species that predate on rodents.

As you think about *time of day*, you realize that this class meets first period on Monday, and just before lunch on Tuesday. In other words, your students face this elevated WM load during the two periods when they might reasonably struggle with WM demands.

As you look over the test you have loved, you also see that it has succumbed to the power of the *Dark Side of the Force*. Because students hadn't done very well in years past, you added more and more *instructions* to give them guidance along the way. However, those instructions themselves might well have become a WM burden. And, you intended to be helpful by giving them many *choices* to write about—Costa Rica, Brazil, Antarctica, etc.—but all those choices might add to your students' cognitive muddle.

(The test itself doesn't include any *technology*, but you have encouraged students to look up scientific names of species when they did their homework—and that multitasking might have led them astray.)

Having reviewed this unit with a WM perspective, in other words, you can quickly understand your students' frustration. Although trophic cascade offers fun mental exercises for ecology experts, it is WM quicksand for people new to the discipline. For that reason, it's not at all surprising that you can, in hindsight, recall several of the *signs and symptoms* of WM overload in last year's class. They often struggled to *process and remember* information; in one memorably horrible class, a student kept losing track of the cause-and-effect cycle of this trophic cascade. When you tried to correct that student, the whole class seemed unusually *unable to focus* on your explanation. And several times, students demonstrated *catastrophic failure*, unable to answer very simple questions about wolves and deer.

How, then, might you solve these WM problems? Given your experience as a teacher, and your review of chapter 3, you see several possible strategies.

Even before you review the list of strategies, you'll probably find yourself making quick decisions to reduce WM load. In the past, for example, you've talked at length about the controversy over reintroducing the wolves to Yellowstone. Now that information feels to you extraneous to the central work of the lesson. Without even realizing that you'd made that decision, you find yourself crossing it off the lesson plan.

When you do review the list of strategies, you can first rely on your students' *long-term memory*. On the test, you will ask them to speculate only about a new top predator in the Costa Rican Cloud Forest; after all, they have studied that environment several times, and its specifics are well lodged in their memories. This strategy also reduces the number of choices they have to make, and so simplifies WM demands that way as well.

Second, you can *redistribute* WM demands across modes. In the past, you have relied on them to come up with their own note-taking strategy to keep track of all these details. This year, instead, you plan to create a graphic template that makes each level of this cascade *visual*. By using up and down arrows, you'll help your students to remember to think about both predator and prey. You will also give them blanks of this form, so they can practice using it to study for the test.

Third, you can *reduce* WM demands by cutting back on the number of species discussed, and the number of scientific names they must memorize. (You briefly contemplate letting them choose which names to memorize, but realize that strategy itself would ramp WM demands back up again.) Rather than give three examples for each step (beaver dams benefit otters, blue herons, and ducks), you'll limit yourself to one or two.

Fourth, you might make a point of *normalizing struggle*. You can, after all, perfectly honestly say that students in years past have found some of these concepts a challenge to take on board, especially because they require imagination and combination. Reassure them that it's normal to feel a little puzzled at first, but that they'll have plenty of time to practice and solidify their understanding.

As you looked over this lesson plan with WM in mind, you almost certainly brought two kinds of analysis to your review. In the first place, you asked yourself specific questions and—when appropriate—settled on well-established strategies. In the second place, you thought about your teaching in a new and different way. You now know facts about WM, and you also know how to think about the relationship between WM and learning. Both your factual knowledge and your ability to think insightfully and flexibly will make immediate and meaningful differences in your students' ability to learn.

It's important to note that these changes make sense *only if the students show WM difficulties.* If you have taught this lesson quite successfully in years past—your students enjoyed it, did well on the test, and demonstrated enduring understanding on the final exam—then you have no need to modify the WM demands. Even without knowing this terminology, clearly you have already found a way to teach the concept within their WM limits. In this case, your review of last year's material will probably show you all the strategies that you successfully employed: strategies that you can use in other units and share with your envious colleagues.

WORKING MEMORY FAQ

1. Although the information presented here makes sense, I confess I'm feeling nervous. If WM overload is as big a problem as you say it is, it seems that we need a radical overhaul of the curriculum. Aren't you basically saying that we need to reduce course content by, say, 50 percent?

Not at all.

If you have been fairly successful in teaching your curriculum when you didn't know about WM, you'll be much more effective now that you do. You might find yourself *redistributing* some of your curriculum to a later part of the unit. But your students will absorb that material more effectively because they can use their WM capacity fully when you do so. You just might be able to cover more content, because your students will learn foundational topics more richly and successfully.

2. Is "multitasking" the same thing as "WM overload"?

Trying to multitask certainly increases the likelihood of WM overload.

When people think they are multitasking, they are in fact rapidly switching back and forth between two different tasks (Lewis-Peacock & Norman, 2014). To accomplish this cognitive work, they have to *remember* what they were doing in task A while *processing* task B, and then—when they switch—remember what they were doing in task B while processing task A. You see right away that *remembering while processing* is a WM challenge.

Especially if tasks A and B are unrelated, this cognitive work is highly ineffective.

3. I've heard that students have seven "slots" in WM, plus or minus two. Why didn't you talk about that?

G.A. Miller (1956) proposed the 7 ± 2 formula decades ago, and it's an interesting place to start. When you tried to alphabetize the five most recent presidents, you could probably do that; if you tried to alphabetize ten, you almost certainly couldn't (unless you teach American history, and have an alphabetical list in long-term memory). However, recent research has moved away from counting "slots," for all sorts of reasons.

First, as we've discussed, students' WM capacity develops during schooling years; seven might be a handy benchmark for adult cognition, but not for seventh graders.

Second, when you were alphabetizing presidents, you were keeping track of more than those names. You had to do some historical contemplation to remember the right presidents, you had to remember how to spell their names, you had to recall the order of the alphabet, and you had to keep track of the instructions. The 7 ± 2 formula applied to only one part of this complex cognitive undertaking—the number of names.

Third, different WM channels have different capacities. Visual WM, for example, seems to be much smaller (Vogel, Woodman, & Luck, 2001).

Rather than counting "slots," attend to WM demands and cognitive success. If your students can do the work, you might ramp up the WM challenge. If they can't, dial it down.

4. Are you absolutely sure we can't increase WM capacity? I keep reading about programs that have shown great promise.

Someday, perhaps, we will figure out how to increase WM. That will be a great day for our species—as important as the printing press for expanding our cognitive potential.

And, scientists have had some successes. Students who lacked early schooling see WM improvements when schooling starts. Patients with brain injuries sometimes respond to treatment to restore some lost WM capacity. As noted below, some techniques help slow the decline of WM as we age.

But truthfully, these few examples—although important for the people involved—don't meet the larger goal: to help people with average WM capacity develop larger-than-average capacity. (Or, said differently, to raise the average capacity for everyone.) We don't know why this kind of training doesn't work, but we do know that the evidence in its favor just isn't very good.

5. But what about those studies that show it does?

WM training programs have been measured in dozens of studies. We should look not at any one study, but at the general message communicated by many studies. And that general message is: we can't do it yet. Truthfully, given how many studies have been done, it would be surprising if none of them showed any positive results.

There's a general lesson here about using psychology research in schools. Teachers and administrators might be inspired and intrigued by one particular study. However, we should always be sure to seek out many other studies that confirm its suggestions. We should also be sure to look for contradictory studies. Without being informed about both sides of a research question, we can't make wise decisions about classroom use of psychology research.

6. What about students with diagnosed WM deficits?

Any student who has a diagnosis should also have an individual plan tailored to that student by an expert. You should follow that plan. Some of that plan's techniques will almost certainly resemble some of the guidance described here, and you will likely understand the reasoning behind those techniques because you have read this book.

The main argument of Part I is that all students—not just those with diagnosed deficits—experience WM overload in school. For that reason, all students will benefit when teachers learn how to anticipate, identify, and solve WM problems.

7. You've said that it's a bad idea for students to take notes on new, complex material. But our students will be taking notes during lecture courses in college. Isn't it our job to prepare them for that work?

If college teachers choose ineffective teaching strategies, that's their responsibility. We shouldn't allow their bad example to force us into bad teaching. In fact, to understand college lectures, our students will need especially strong foundation in our disciplines. We should therefore adopt the best possible teaching strategies now to give our students a fighting chance in college.

It's important to note, of course, that some college professors understand the inadequacy of simple lecture. These professors, dedicated to their craft and their discipline, work hard and work imaginatively to ensure that their classes—even their lectures—require active cognitive participation and thus foster learning. The best college lecturers, in fact, might serve as models for our own work.

8. That closing summary was helpful, but I'm not an ecology teacher. Can you give me a list that's tailored more precisely to my own classroom?

You might use department or grade-level meetings to discuss WM strategies that fit best in your context. Shared teacherly wisdom can solve many seemingly insoluble problems.

Cognitive science can provide teachers with helpful principles of learning. Because each classroom is different—different students, different school culture, different curriculum, different teacher—the application of those principles will always vary from classroom to classroom. And the teacher is always the best person to translate those principles—no one knows your students or yourself as well as you do.

9. You keep saying I should use my instincts. But I'm a first-year teacher, so I don't have well-developed teaching instincts. What advice do you have for me?

First, welcome to the profession. For many of us, nothing is more rewarding than helping youngsters grow into good and thoughtful people. Teaching is a wonderful way to spend your professional life.

Second, give yourself a little credit. If you want to be a teacher, you've probably been watching teachers for a while, and noticing which techniques do and don't work—at least for students like you. If you've been noticing your own learning, you've been developing instincts about teaching.

Third, be systematic about the steps above. When you put a lesson plan together, take time to review it with the *anticipate* strategies in mind. When a colleague visits your class, ask her to look for *signs and symptoms* of catastrophic failure. Be deliberate about *making information visual*. You've got lots of strategies for managing your students' WM health.

Fourth, protect your own WM by limiting your efforts. If you try to think about everything, you'll overwhelm your own cognitive capacity. Each week, choose a particular topic or skill that merits your attention; perhaps your department head or mentor teacher can guide you. If, for example, you choose to focus on *normalizing struggle* this week, then next week you can pick one of the attention strategies that will be discussed in Part II of this book.

10. You've said that dividing WM load between visual and auditory channels reduces the likelihood of overload. What about the kinesthetic channel?

Advice about visual and verbal channels sounds similar to learning styles theories, especially those that emphasize "verbal, auditory, and kinesthetic learners." However, it comes instead from Baddeley's model of WM function (2003). This model includes visual and auditory components, but does not include a "kinesthetic channel." In fact, very little research has been done into anything that might plausibly be called "kinesthetic WM." (Sian Beilock and Susan Goldin-Meadow have done interesting work about using gesture to facilitate learning (Beilock, 2015; Goldin-Meadow & Beilock, 2010); however, they never describe such gestures as a kind of WM.)

By the way, learning styles theory is quite controversial. Although a great many teachers find such theories persuasive (Dekker, Lee, Howard-Jones, & Jolles, 2012), psychology research routinely discredits them (Pashler, McDaniel, Rohrer, & Bjork, 2008; Willingham, 2009).

11. What about my own WM? Honestly, it's feeling a little rusty as I get older.

I feel your pain.

When we talk about cognitive science, we can fall into the bad habit of describing the brain as a free-standing object. However, we have lots of very persuasive research suggesting that the brain is *a part of the body*. It is, in fact, *physically attached* to the body. For this reason, everything that is bad for bodies is bad for brains—including aging. As we get older, we don't sleep as well as we used to, and we can't lift such heavy things anymore, and we get just a little bit more forgetful. And, our WM capacity does go down somewhat.

12. Is there anything we can do to prevent this decline, or at least slow it down?

Just as everything that is bad for bodies is bad for brains, so too everything that is good for bodies is good for brains. Mental and physical exercise, good nutrition, and sleep can help various cognitive functions. And we do have some evidence of long-term benefits—especially for mental and physical exercise.

Here's another thing you can do: be forgiving with yourself. If you can't alphabetize lists as quickly as you used to, that's normal. (It is, in fact, more normal than boasting about alphabetizing skills in the first place.) All the techniques that help your students will help you as well. Make lists. Learn routines. Create mnemonics. Simplify tasks. If you can anticipate WM challenges in your own life, and identify the symptoms when you feel them, you've got plenty of strategies for solving those problems.

Part II

ATTENTION

Chapter Five

Redefining Attention

Imagine a fresh scenario:

Walking down a Boston street, sipping away at your coffee, you see a baffled stranger peering at a piece of paper. "How do I get to Skyline Park?" he asks, squinting at directions. As you start to think your way through this question, two people—bizarrely, carrying a sheet of plywood—walk between you two and briefly interrupt your view. (On Boston sidewalks, any kind of oddness seems plausible.) During this momentary interruption, you figure out this stranger's best route—the park, after all, is just a few short blocks away. After you point out essential landmarks, he thanks you and sets off down the street. You walk on, feeling good about your random act of kindness, and about the warmth of your java.

Here's the surprising part of this story. The man to whom you gave directions was, in fact, not the man who initially asked you the question. While your view was blocked, the original stranger switched places with one of the people carrying the plywood. You didn't even notice the change. When confronted with that embarrassing reality, you just might spill your coffee.

If you're skeptical such a thing could happen, go online and look up "Inside Nova's" episode on change blindness (www.pbs.org/wgbh/nova/body/change-blindness.html). You'll see several people miss the switcheroo, and cheerfully offer directions to someone they've never spoken to before. In both this video and in Daniel Simons's famous research on change blindness, roughly half the people don't notice obvious switches happening right before their eyes (Simons & Levin, 1998).

This plywood scenario feels strangely familiar to teachers. On some days, we might as well vanish behind plywood and turn into a mysterious stranger—our students would barely notice.

EXPLAINING DISTRACTION: PROBLEMS
AND SOLUTIONS

In any faculty room, you hear this lament: "Why don't my students just *pay attention*?!"

That question comes right from the heart. You spent weeks this summer putting together a syllabus incorporating the latest techniques. You devoted all of Saturday to constructing an inspiring lesson plan. You taught today's class with an élan that the Ringling Brothers would admire. All you ask is that your students pay attention, and they don't even do that. How much more can you possibly do?

As you recall this profound frustration, so common to every teacher's experience, try this two-step exercise.

First, imagine that you ask your students this question: "Why is it hard to pay attention in class?" How would they answer you? Take a moment to jot down their answers. (We'll come back to this list later in the chapter, so be sure to keep your response close by.)

Your students' answers will differ depending on your specific circumstances: the grade and subject you teach, the school where you work, the persona you bring to the classroom. But no matter the circumstance, you can probably rattle off several answers with ease.

A representative list might look like this:

- It's hot in here.
- Everything happened so fast.
- He's bothering me.
- I'm hungry.
- The noise in the hall makes it hard to concentrate.
- I don't understand.
- I'm tired.
  And the most dreaded answer:
- It's just so *boooooring* … (You might add an eye-roll to this answer for extra effect.)

Step two of this exercise: ask yourself, how would you and your colleagues answer the same question? As you look at your students' lives, what makes attention difficult for them? Again, take a minute to add to your list.

When asked this question, teachers typically identify many problems:

- She just didn't get enough sleep last night.
- Today's technology trains students to change focus too often. All that chatting and tweeting.

- Look at what that kid is wearing; no wonder no one can pay attention.
- It's just not normal and healthy for kids to sit still so long. Can we please give them recess again?

Headline #1: both students and teachers can quickly identify several potential *problems* with attention. Headline #2: because we know what the problems are, we seek out some new set of *solutions*.

Yet, once teachers begin to understand psychology and neuroscience research, we realize that we have those headlines more-or-less backward. In fact, *we fundamentally misunderstand our students' problems with attention*. And, once we understand them, it turns out that *we already have many effective solutions* right at hand.

Our students do not have problems with attention. In fact, when you missed the switcheroo behind the plywood, you didn't have an attention problem either. To understand this striking claim, it helps to imagine a construction site.

Across the street from your school, someone has bought a plot of land to build a house. Each day, men and women wearing hard hats and toting daunting tools show up and make all sorts of noise. As the weeks go by, a structure rises out of the ground, and you can't help but admire the house and the people who built it.

From the observer's point of view, it makes sense to speak of "the people who built the house." From the participants' point of view, however, *no one really built a house*. One group of specialists came in and laid a foundation. Another group came in and put up a frame. More specialists arrived: HVAC technicians and plumbers and electricians and roofers and painters. Although a house was built, no one really built a house. Instead, each of the specialists created specific parts, and *those parts came together to create a greater whole*.

Scientists think about attention the same way. Attention is the house created by cognitive subprocesses, but no one of those cognitive subprocesses creates attention. Each subprocess contributes an essential element, and those elements come together to create a greater whole: attention (Posner & Rothbart, 2006; Raz & Buhle, 2006).

For this reason, teachers need to rethink our own efforts to help students pay attention. We have been thinking of attention as one whole thing and have been insisting that our students pay it. Understanding attention in this new way, we now realize we must focus on those cognitive subprocesses. If we help our students accomplish those subtasks, the result will be attention. But we needn't emphasize attention; we should emphasize the parts that will come together to make a beautiful, attentive whole.

ATTENTION REDEFINED

This shift in perspective can be quite jarring. For as long as we've been in school, and certainly as long as we have been teaching, attention has been an essential goal in our work. And yet attention can't be achieved by reaching directly for it. Teachers can foster our students' attention only by focusing on these other neural subprocesses.

To start thinking about attention as researchers do, teachers need to answer three questions:

1. What are those subprocesses that create attention?
2. What do problems with these subprocesses look like in our classrooms? In other words, how can we distinguish one from another?
3. Once we can identify these problems, what can teachers do to promote each of these processes?

Answers to the first two questions—definitions and classroom examples—follow in this chapter. Answers to the third question—how do we foster each of these subprocesses—require greater exploration in chapters 6–8. Happily, answers to all three questions suggest practical and immediate changes that we can make in our classrooms and schools. After all, although attention isn't one neural process, the House of Attention is very real indeed. When we build it, one subprocess at a time, we foster student learning.

Like all scientific theories, this understanding of attention has a long and fascinating history. Throughout the twentieth century, many scientists proposed models for attention (Raz & Buhle, 2006). In 1971, Michael Posner and Stephen Boies first outlined a theory that has come to be scientific consensus: attention is a combination of three distinct neural processes. The labels for those processes have changed over the years. (In truth, terminology in this field can be confusing, even contradictory.) For the sake of simplicity, we will use widely accepted terminology: *alertness*, *orienting*, and *executive attention* (EA).

Alertness

In the brain sciences, definitions can sometimes be tricky. For example, when a neuroscientist uses the word "transfer," she means something quite different from what an educational psychologist means. As we saw in chapter 2, "cognitive disinhibition" is the excessively fancy label for thinking about familiar topics in unusual ways.

Happily, when attention researchers talk about *alertness*, they mean what you and I mean: Is this particular student awake at all? Awake enough? Or, perhaps, too awake? Bouncing around like Spiderman on a sugar high?

Defining alertness is easy; so too describing classroom problems with alertness. A few minutes ago, when you listed attention problems (or, problems that you once thought of as attention problems), several examples were probably alertness problems. The student is dozing? That's a low-alertness problem. The student is scampering around the room, wielding a pair of open scissors? That's a high-alertness problem.

Even at this stage, it helps to draw a clear distinction: the sleeping student and the scissors-wielding student do *not* need us to help them with attention, because—as we have seen—attention results from multiple subprocesses. Those students *do* need us to help them with alertness, for the right level of alertness will help them build the House of Attention.

Orienting

Students absorb information through their senses. They can see things, hear things, touch things, and so forth. Phrased in more technical language, they perceive environmental stimuli.

On the one hand, such perception grounds all learning. Students can't learn what we want to teach if they haven't seen the new conjugation on the board, heard the instructions we have spoken, manipulated the microscope just so. On the other hand, perception can distract from learning because—here is a crucial point—at every second, the environment includes vastly more stimuli than we can ever perceive. As you read this page right now, you are probably not perceiving the color of the ceiling overhead, or the background hum of the air conditioner, or the tension in your left ankle. When you read that sentence, you abruptly perceived those stimuli—but, of course, they were there all along.

This neural limitation explains the second element of attention: *orienting*. Our students must not only be alert enough to perceive but must also *orient to the appropriate environmental stimuli*. A student absorbed with the bird outside the window, or contemplating the attractive person sitting right over there, or praying for a bathroom break may be alert, but is so disoriented that no learning takes place.

When you listed reasons that students struggle to pay attention, you almost certainly listed several orienting problems. Because students do not orient to you or to the work they should be doing, they struggle to learn. Here again, we must keep in mind that these are not attention problems, but orienting problems. Attention results when alert students orient to classroom material.

Executive Attention

Here's a fun task to try. You'll need to time yourself, so have some kind of stopwatch handy.

In figure 5.1, you see twenty pairs of numbers. Your remarkably simple goal: point to the number in each pair that has the *higher value*. If you see a 3 and a 7, you would point to the 7 because 7 has a higher value than 3. You strive to be as fast and accurate as possible, so once you've got your stopwatch ready, you can GO!

3 5	8 4	6 7	9 5	2 1
22 15	66 64	21 61	46 52	17 19
8 9	6 4	3 2	1 7	5 8
37 34	43 47	25 52	76 83	88 91

Figure 5.1   Self-Test #1.

Write down how many seconds that took you, because you're about to compete with yourself. With figure 5.2, you should do exactly the same thing a second time: go through the pairs of numbers, pointing to the number that has the higher value. Remember, of course, to keep track of your time. As before, you want to be both fast and accurate. Our research question: how much faster will you get with practice? Let's find out: GO!

3 5	8 4	**6 7**	9 **5**	**2** 1
22 15	66 **64**	21 **61**	**46 52**	**17** 19
8 9	**6** 4	3 **2**	1 7	**5 8**
37 34	**43** 47	25 52	**76** 83	88 **91**

Figure 5.2   Self-Test #2.

How much faster did you accomplish the second task? For almost everyone, the second list is in fact harder and takes more time (Henik & Tzelgov, 1982). Here's why:

When you saw the pairs in figure 5.1, you could concentrate solely on the value of the number. Even in first grade you could easily recognize that 5 is greater than 3. When you processed the pairs in figure 5.2, however, you had to juggle competing sets of information. 5 is larger than 3 if you concentrate on the value of the numbers. But—depending on which pair your examined— the 3 might be larger than the 5 in its physical size. Faced with this extra level of cognitive work, you had to resolve a mental conflict between your impulses. This extra work took more time.

As you resolved this conflict in your brain, you could probably feel the extra effort you put into the second task. That effort is, in fact, the third and final element of attention. Researchers call it *executive attention*, and that phrase describes *voluntary, effortful control of cognitive processes.*

Although teachers can easily envision alertness and orienting problems in class, we struggle to identify executive attention problems. A sleeping student? Alertness problem. A student tapping away at a text message? Orienting problem. But how do we recognize executive attention problems?

We will discuss this difficult question at length in chapter 8. For the time being, the simplest shorthand is this: when students *seem to think about a problem the wrong way*, you are probably witnessing an executive attention problem.

Here's an example. In your English class, after a brisk grammar review, you ask Jacob to read the first practice sentence in the book. You want him to identify the part of speech for the word "poodle." Jacob looks down at the book, looks back up at you, and says hesitantly, "metaphor?" You want to cry out: "Metaphor? Jacob, PAY ATTENTION." But, at that very moment, you remember that attention is more than just one thing.

Was Jacob having an alertness problem? Not at all. He was appropriately alert, neither dozing nor racing about the room.

Was he having an orienting problem? Again, no. He didn't look out the window, or at a classmate, or at his phone. He took in the correct stimuli from the environment: the instructions you gave, and then the sample sentence from the book.

Instead, Jacob had an executive attention problem. He wasn't managing his own thinking processes correctly. You asked him for a *part* of speech. But, "metaphor" is never a part of speech; it's a *figure* of speech. Trying to juggle lots of information, he ended up grabbing almost randomly at an answer that simply made no sense.

When students choose a chemistry formula to solve a physics problem, or put a noun ending on a verb in Spanish, or use an example from the Shang

Dynasty to make a point about Japanese history—in all these cases, they are not effectively controlling their cognitive processes. Their executive attention has let them down.

An important note: teachers reasonably enough wonder about the relationship between *executive attention* and *executive function*. Briefly, executive attention is one of many executive functions. Working memory, prioritizing, task initiation, inhibition: cognitive scientists group these abilities together as executive functions, and executive attention belongs in this group. (Different writers have different lists of executive functions, so don't worry if yours varies from this one.)

To recap: when students are appropriately alert (neither asleep nor crazed with energy), when they orient to the correct classroom stimuli (and not to some off-topic distraction), and when they contemplate those stimuli as we want them to (not with some randomly inappropriate cognitive process), then they are building the House of Attention. If any of those subprocesses go awry, they no longer pay attention. But we can't restore attention by asking for it. Instead, we need to fix the underlying problem.

AN ESSENTIAL NEW TEACHING SKILL

Posner's tripartite structure offers teachers an essential framework for understanding our classes, our students, and our frustrations. Without this scientific framework, we think we know what the problem is (the students aren't paying attention), but we don't know what the solutions might be. The truth, however, is just the opposite. We already know many of the solutions; in fact, some suggestions that follow in chapters 6–8 will sound comfortably familiar. However, we don't know what the problem is, because we mistake an alertness problem (or an orienting problem, or an executive attention problem) for an attention problem—and, as we now know, attention is more than one thing.

Imagine for a moment that, because of your exceptional coaching, your soccer team has reached the league finals. After a week of intensive practice, you gather your squad on the sidelines to give your pregame pep talk: "Girls," you say, "here's our strategy. I want you to go out there, and I want you to *win the game*. That's our strategy today: *win the game*." An awkward pause follows. The girls glance at each other nervously and shuffle their cleats. At last, the team captain speaks up: "Coach," she says, "*win the game* isn't a strategy. *Win the game* is the goal. We already know what the goal is. We need you to tell us how to do it. That's what a strategy would be." She is, of course, right.

Every time we tell our students to *pay attention*, we are reminding them of the goal. But they already know what the goal is. They know that they are supposed to pay attention. In order to meet that goal, they need to succeed at three different mental processes: alertness *and* orienting *and* executive attention. But telling them to "pay attention" doesn't tell them which one of those processes isn't currently working. And it doesn't tell them how to kick start the process either. Our primary strategy for helping students pay attention— telling them to "pay attention"—is basically useless.

For this reason, Posner's scientific understanding of attention requires teachers to develop an essential new skill: *diagnosis*. We need to distinguish alertness problems from orienting problems, and both of those from executive attention problems. Until we do so, we keep treating them all alike, and our solutions will work only by accident. After all, an alertness solution won't solve an orienting problem. In fact, our alertness solution could make that orienting problem worse.

Like all teaching skills, this new diagnostic skill requires practice. Most teachers have spent years, even decades, identifying attention problems—not realizing that we were falsely lumping together three distinct classroom difficulties. Because diagnosis is such an important skill, we should devote real time to practicing it.

Diagnostic Practice #1

At the beginning of this chapter, you made two lists of classroom problems: one that your students might identify, and another that you and your colleagues might identify. Pause now and return to that list. For each problem that you listed, ask yourself:

- Is this a problem with energy level? Is the student too energetic, or not enough? In this case, you have identified an *alertness* problem.
- Is this a problem with focus? Are my students perceiving the right environmental stimuli—the work we are doing in class—or are they distracted by other stimuli? In this case, they have an *orienting* problem.
- Is this a problem with effortful control of thought? Are my students, grabbing haphazardly at strange answers, seeming to think about the problem in the wrong way? Here you have spotted an *executive attention* problem.

Your list may include one or two examples that leave you puzzled. If you get stuck, think of a very specific example of it—recall the last time you faced that particular problem in class. With that fresh example in mind, review the bullet points above. If this approach doesn't fully solve the puzzle, don't worry. The rest of part II will offer more examples, and that discussion will help you contemplate this question anew.

Diagnostic Practice #2

In a moment of hyperbole, I just claimed that saying "pay attention"—our primary strategy to help our students build their Attention House—is basically useless. In fact, telling students to pay attention probably does help with at least one of these three subprocesses. (If it were truly useless, teachers wouldn't have been doing it for so long.)

Take a moment to ask yourself: which one or two of the subprocesses get at least a temporary boost when we tell students to "pay attention"?

Here are the answers I hear most often. The longer that they attend school, the more our students understand that—in Posner's language—"pay attention" means "orient to me." When teachers say "pay attention," students look up from their phones, down from the ceiling fan, away from the ice-cream truck outside and toward the teacher.

Secondarily, "pay attention" might help with alertness levels. A dozing student knows to perk up a bit, while a scampering student knows to calm down for the moment.

The great failing of this strategy is that it focuses on the symptom, not the underlying problem. Students disoriented by an ice-cream truck may be able to refocus on you for a determined minute. However, as long as that truck remains in their line of sight, it will be a potential and powerful source of disorientation.

We will discuss solutions to these problems in upcoming chapters. For now, we are practicing thinking about attention in this new way.

Diagnostic Practice #3

As a third way to practice diagnosing attention problems, think back to the plywood switcheroo on the streets of Boston. A stranger asked you for directions. You gave those directions to a different stranger, and you never noticed the change. If a friend had watched all this from across the street, she might be amazed at your oversight: "How did you not notice that there were two different guys? You need to learn to pay attention!"

Now that you know more about attention science than your well-meaning but ill-informed friend, try to diagnose the problem as Posner might. Put down this book for a minute and ask yourself: Did you fall short on alertness, orienting, or executive attention?

Most teachers, when they think their way through this question, arrive at the following answer:

In this case, you have not shown an alertness problem. After all, you—or the people in the video—are obviously functionally awake. You haven't fallen asleep on the sidewalk. You haven't raced past the stranger in a caffeine-induced frenzy.

Likewise, you aren't showing signs of an executive attention problem. You thought about the problem in the correct way. When asked for directions, you perhaps looked at his piece of paper, or peered up at the street signs, or turned inward to contemplate a mental map. All of these strategies could help answer this stranger's question. You did not produce an oddly off-topic answer. If you had taken out a cook book, or offered up $20, or even said "call Uber," you would not have been thinking about the problem correctly. ("Call Uber" would be a helpful answer if the park were at a greater distance. Given that it's just a few blocks away, Uber seems like an odd strategy indeed.) Your thought processes wouldn't be addressing the question you'd been asked.

Instead, you have failed to *orient* to a key stimulus in the environment: the stranger's face. Because you did not orient to that stimulus—in other words, because you didn't look at him closely—you failed to notice the switch.

Recall that your friend diagnosed you as having an attention problem. When she scolded you for not paying attention, you might retort in anger: "What do you mean I wasn't paying attention? He asked for directions, and I gave him excellent directions. Of course I was paying attention!" This angry retort makes a reasonable point. This stranger gave you a particular mission, a particular homework assignment, and you accomplished that mission effectively and generously. Bizarrely, the stranger then tested you on a completely different assignment: facial recognition. Although you failed that test, you have reason to cry foul. After all, the facial-recognition test was never on the syllabus.

Two key points emerge from this imaginary exchange. First, notice how easily the environment disoriented you. Although the stranger's face was right in front of you, you automatically oriented to the paper instead and therefore missed a perfectly obvious fact in the environment. When you contemplate your students' academic lives, you can see how easily they too might be disoriented. As teachers, we know which one or two of the environmental stimuli merit their focus. That is, we know that students should listen to me, not the squeaky locker in the hallway. They should concentrate on the problem they are solving, not on that odd, faint reek of formaldehyde. However, students struggle to recognize our priorities and therefore can quite easily miss the central points that are so obvious to us. In this way, Posner's framework helps us understand some of our students' baffling lapses.

Second, notice that the word "attention" didn't help elucidate the problem. When your friend scolded you for failing to pay attention, you reacted with perfectly reasonable anger. You had indeed been paying attention and been quite generous in doing so. Her guidance didn't benefit you; it started an argument. (Perhaps this imaginary argument resembles others you have had with your students, when they insisted—despite obvious evidence to the contrary—that they were paying attention.)

If, however, your friend read up on the science of attention, she might have spoken specifically and helpfully about a particular subprocess: "When you started looking at the paper, you didn't orient to the first man's face, and so you didn't notice the exchange behind the plywood. Next time a stranger asks for directions, be sure to get a good look at him before you answer his question." In this case, your friend's advice correctly diagnoses the problem, and offers a useful solution—one that ensures no one will be able to vanish behind plywood when you're in charge.

To sum up, For as long as teachers have been teaching, we have been frustrated by our students' inattention. We recognize the gravity of the problem every day, and yet we can't quite find the right set of solutions.

However, once we understand attention research, we realize that we have in fact deeply misunderstood the root of the problem. We have been striving heroically but vainly to solve a problem that doesn't exist in the form we thought it did. Falsely lumping together alertness, orienting, and executive attention, we've been treating symptoms without solving underlying cognitive problems.

Once we retrain ourselves with the new skill of diagnosis, we can determine if our students are having problems with alertness, orienting, or executive attention. And having diagnosed this underlying problem, we are dramatically likelier to find the right solution. This kind of retraining takes time, but the immediacy of the results makes that effort worthwhile. What are the solutions to these problems? Chapters 6–8 reveal all …

Chapter Six

Alertness

In chapter 5, we listed three questions that teachers need to answer:

1. What are the subprocesses that create attention?
2. What do problems with these subprocesses look like in our classrooms? How can we distinguish one from another?
3. Once we can identify these problems, what can teachers do to promote each of these processes?

Now that we have answered the first two questions, we turn to the third. Once we diagnose a classroom situation as an alertness, orienting, or executive attention problem, how do we solve it? Better still, can we anticipate these problems and prevent them from happening in the first place?

VISUALIZING THE ATTENTIONAL FIELD

To answer these essential questions, it helps to visualize the relationship among these processes. Figure 6.1 represents our students' *attentional field*: that is, all the subprocesses that come together to produce attention (based on T. Rose, personal communication, October 11, 2011). On the left in figure 6.1, we see several environmental stimuli. With literally thousands of things to look at, listen to, and touch, a student might stare at a classmate, or notice the rumbling in his stomach, or hear the ping of a text message. In some rare and happy cases, that student might orient to the school work at hand. At every moment, we can graph the particular power a stimulus has in this student's attentional field. (As seen on the top axis, the higher the bar, the more salient the stimulus.)

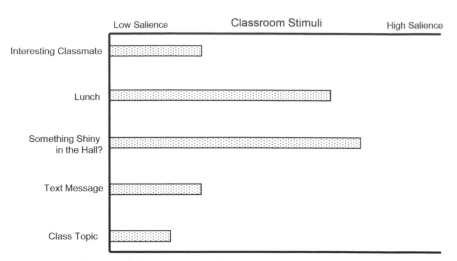

Figure 6.1   Salience of Classroom Stimuli.

The student in figure 6.1 focuses mostly on the shiny thing in the hallway. Lunch comes in second. The topic being discussed in class comes in a distant fifth place. For this student, the shiny thing is the most salient stimulus, whereas the class topic is the least.

So far, this figure emphasizes the *orienting* element of attention. At this particular moment, this student orients to sparkly things and food, but does not orient to text messages. We can add *alertness* to the bottom axis of this graph, as seen in figure 6.2.

When we add a line indicating the student's moderate alertness level, we create a kind of *attention threshold.* At present, only two of the environmental stimuli clear that threshold: the shiny hallway trinket and food. In other words, this student is consciously aware of two parts of his world. He isn't really aware of anything else—not, for example, quadratic equations, or the Peloponnesian War, or words that rhyme with "hat."

As we know, alertness levels can change. A student who arrived in class well-rested yesterday may be sleep-deprived today. Such changes, in turn, alter the number of stimuli that cross the student's alertness threshold. At the very low alertness level in figure 6.3, no stimuli penetrate his fog of exhaustion. (Notice that, counterintuitively, a low level of alertness is on right of this figure.) This student might as well be sleeping.

Even at this very low alertness level, it might be possible for a stimulus to cross the student's alertness threshold. If the fire alarm went off, or if the latest chart-topping pop-star walked by, that particular stimulus just might be salient enough. For the time being, however, no learning is taking place.

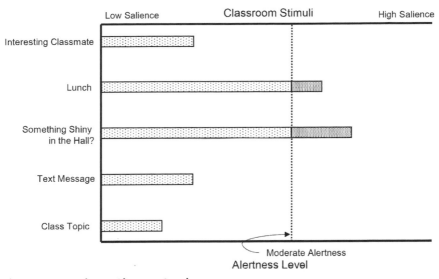

Figure 6.2 Moderate Alertness Level.

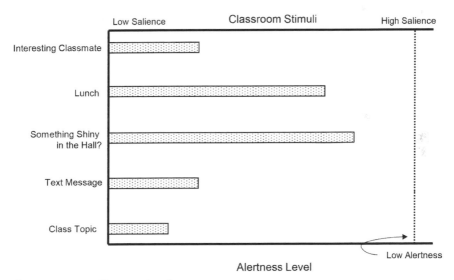

Figure 6.3 Low Alertness Level.

Conversely, the very high alertness level in figure 6.4 means that *all* these stimuli cross the threshold. Because this student is hyperactively alert, like a young child ready to open birthday presents, incoming information simply overwhelms effective cognitive processing.

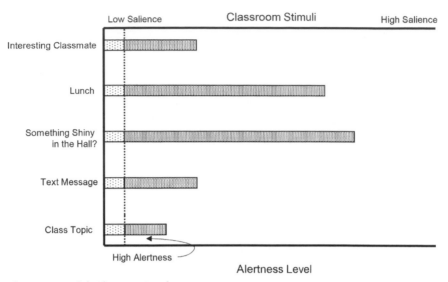

Figure 6.4 High Alertness Level.

Clearly, both low and high alertness levels preclude learning. For this reason, teachers strive—as our first goal—to *moderate our students' alertness levels.*

ALERTNESS SOLUTIONS

When we diagnose an alertness problem, teachers have at least four research-aligned solutions to moderate students' baseline energy levels. To understand these strategies, we will discuss cunning leopards, hapless researchers, drowsy judges, and conference presenters.

Mind the Leopard

Let's rewind human history about 200,000 years to the dawn of *Homo sapiens.* A group of us wake up one morning in our cave, and I am the first one outside to greet the new dawn. In front of me I see some trees. I love those trees. They were there yesterday. In the distance I see the river where we fish. I love that river. It was there yesterday. Off to the side I see a rock in the scrub. That rock was *not* there yesterday. In fact, that rock is moving. Now that I'm focused on it, I can see that the rock is a leopard, coming straight at me ...

In just a few moments, I will no longer be a potential ancestor for future people. My particular gene pool will stop with me. Note that my fellow *Homo sapiens* don't need to be faster than the leopard; they need to be faster than I am (Ridley, 1993). And because I am so focused on the lovable tree and river, I don't notice the new rock/leopard off to the side until it is too late. The others in my group notice the new rock right away, and because they spot it before I do, they live to hunt another day. In other words, they survive because they *alert to visual novelty*. However sleepy they still are, they wake right up when an unfamiliar object appears in their field of vision.

We can humorously summarize evolutionary pressures in three simple questions: Can it eat me? Can I eat it? Is this an opportunity for reproduction? If I am the first one of my group to spot a predator, or a potential meal, or a tempting mate, my genes are that much likelier to survive to the next generation. In other words, we all inherited our genes from ancestors who alerted to visual novelty—all of us, including our students (Medina, 2008; see also Posner & Rothbart, 2006, for a neurobiological account).

This leopard story seems to highlight the orienting component of attention, because my cave mates looked right at the leopard. Although subtle, the effect on alertness is more important for teachers to understand. Even though my adult cave mates were quite sleepy, they immediately woke up when their brains registered a potential threat in peripheral vision. My cave mates' children might have been cavorting as they came out of the cave, but they quieted right down when they registered a threat. When they perceived visual novelty, their alertness levels immediately changed.

Because visual novelty has such power to moderate our students' alertness levels, teachers can use it either to wake our sleepy students up or calm our energetic ones down. Imagine, for instance, that you look at an old lesson plan and remember that last year's students lost energy about halfway through. This year, you can make sure to introduce visual novelty at that time. Have a slide show ready. Give them some photographs to analyze. Reveal a new poster and have them decide where it belongs in the room.

Sometimes, teachers face students who are predictably dazed at the beginning of class. Because most high schools start classes far too early in the morning (Kelley, Lockley, Foster, & Kelley, 2015), high school teachers often despair to raise our students' alertness during first period. Knowing about the power of visual novelty, you might—for example—rearrange the furniture in the room. For the same reason that my *Homo sapiens* cave mates alerted to that leopard, your students will alert to the new layout of the classroom.

In all these cases, videos are your friend. High school teachers facing cranky, sleep-deprived teens at 7:30 in the morning might begin class with high-energy videos: pogo-stick stunts, extreme bicyclists racing down mountain sides, quirky music videos with swirls of technicolor paint. True enough, this approach subtracts a minute or two from class time, and for this reason might seem like a bad idea. However, such antics reliably perk teen-aged students right up. When you get to work at 7:32, therefore, your class will have dramatically more energy and clarity than they otherwise would have done. In other words, this teaching strategy schedules a minute or two for raising alertness levels and thereby makes your discussion of Shakespeare, or the chain rule, or magnetic fields dramatically more meaningful.

Because videos do such a good job of promoting visual novelty, teachers can use them to present content as well. Teachers have always known that professionally produced videos enliven classes. We can use even short clips to the same effect. In fact, many websites make it quite easy for nonexperts— even technophobes—to put alertness-generating videos together. Such websites as Animoto.com and EDPuzzle.com allow teachers either to create videos or to edit and annotate videos quite simply. Doubtless you can discover many other such products. Using these technologies, you can simultaneously present content and moderate your students' alertness. Win–win.

Whether you feel drawn to redecorating the classroom, rearranging the desks, or resplicing a video, remember that alertness to visual novelty saved our ancestor from predators, and can save our students from alertness imbalance.

10 Minutes, and Beyond ...

For several years now, the "Ten Minute Rule" has floated around teaching conferences and been advocated in teaching manuals (Medina, 2008). According to this rule, people can attend for ten minutes before they start to lose focus. Effective teachers, therefore, should change something up every ten minutes or so, presumably to refresh alertness. This "rule" has several formulations, some accounting for age, some factoring in intrinsic motivation, and some others—doubtless—dividing by pi.

By hunting down footnotes and references, Karen Wilson and James Korn (2007) have tried to find the research basis for this advice. The answer: not so much.

Attention researchers, as Wilson and Korn help explain, face a difficult question: how can we know that a person is in fact paying attention? In many cases, we might know who is not paying attention: the person staring out the window may well have her attention elsewhere. However, the student looking at me and taking notes might be faking attention convincingly. (I once took a college class so dull that I wrote letters simply to stay awake. I glanced up at the lecturer occasionally to be polite.) In other words, although researchers might know who isn't paying attention, we struggle to know who is.

Wilson and Korn's historical investigation found that the "Ten Minute Rule" derives primarily from well-meaning but not terribly reliable research. In some cases, researchers visited lecture halls and timed the onset of "a period of general lack of concentration involving the majority of the class, and not merely isolated individuals" (Wilson & Korn, 2007, p. 86). However, they measured this onset time simply by scanning the room. As a research method, this approach hardly qualifies as scientific.

After all, an experienced doctor may look at an individual patient and be quite certain she has a fever. But that doctor will always use a thermometer to take an objective measurement. And, no doctor would ever survey a waiting room of patients and say: "well, several of them look feverish, so I think I'll prescribe them all antibiotics." Worthwhile psychology relies on individual measurements of specific variables, not general group hunches. (By the way, even with such "hunchy" measurements, the onset time for inattention varied widely, depending on the class and the instructor.)

In other words, teachers already know that students lose focus over time. We know that their minds are likelier to wander the longer they do one thing. This common-sense knowledge makes highly specific rules delivered by confident professionals—"a six-year-old can attend for only six minutes!"—feel persuasive and helpful. Yet these prescriptions lack solid research, and might well lead us to adopt counter-productive strategies. Guidance gleaned from general observations of college lectures should neither prescribe nor proscribe teaching practices in K–12 classrooms (Rodriguez & Fitzpatrick, 2014).

Researcher Diane Bunce has tried to solve the attention measurement problem by using classroom clickers (Bunce, Flens, & Neiles, 2010). In this study, Bunce and her colleagues worked with students enrolled in three different sections of a chemistry class: chemistry for engineering majors, organic chemistry for nursing majors, and general chemistry for nonmajors. In each group, participants were instructed to press a button on a clicker when they realized that they had not been paying attention. By using these clickers, Bunce's team gathered specific data about individual students, not general impressions about a lecture hall. (Of course, her method relied on her participants' honesty and self-awareness.) To ensure a very broad sample size, the researchers tracked these three classes for over a month.

Bunce's study revealed several important flaws with the "Ten Minute Rule." First, these three classes showed dramatically different attentional patterns over the first several minutes of the lecture. Among the nonmajors, the self-identified inattention rate ranged from less than 5 percent to 35 percent; among the nurses taking organic chemistry, it ranged from 15 percent to 70 percent. While researchers could find a mathematical average to all these numbers, that average would disguise an essential finding: attention rates varied substantially between these two classes. In other words, an average exists, but it would offer teachers no meaningful guidance (Rose, 2016). Note, too, inattention rose and fell quite frequently, even in the first few minutes of class. Different sections of these chemistry classes saw inattentional peaks at three minutes, five minutes, seven minutes, and—yes—about ten minutes. Simply put: the "Ten Minute Rule" isn't a rule, and it doesn't last ten minutes.

Although Bunce's study seems to offer only gloomy conclusions—college students can't stay focused for even a few minutes!—these clicker classes do help us promote our students' alertness. Bunce's team tracked not only time, but also the professor's *actions* during the class. This second set of measurements showed a simple way to reduce inattention rates: stop lecturing and *do something else*. Specifically, Bunce found that when professors stopped either to answer questions or to do a chemistry demonstration, this change of pace halved the inattention rate for five minutes after the lecture resumed. You read that right. Simply stopping to do something more interactive cut the inattention rate in half.

This particular strategy isn't a surprise; almost any teacher, noticing an alertness problem in my class, would advise me to switch to a new activity. (Notice, by the way, that "doing a chemistry demonstration" is a new activity that also introduces visual novelty.) However, the Bunce study helps teachers both by offering clear research support for this common-sense strategy and by putting the "Ten Minute Rule" out of our misery.

The end of the "Ten Minute Rule" has an important flip side as well. Montessori schools instruct teachers to leave focused children alone. If your students are working productively for long stretches of time—that is, if their alertness levels have not flagged despite the passage of twenty minutes—you should not let any teaching "rule" force you to interrupt them. The first step in fostering attention is diagnosing the problem; if there is no problem, the teacher (like Hippocrates) should do no harm.

Justice is Blind and Tired

In theory, we find comfort in the notion that the law is no respecter of persons. Evenhandedly unaware of a defendant's identity, the legal system decides a case not on status, family, income, or fame, but on the facts alone. To test this hypothesis in the Israeli judicial system, Shai Danziger and his research team studied parole decisions made by experienced judges—judges, that is, with an average of over twenty years on the bench (Danziger, Levav, & Avnaim-Pesso, 2011).

In theory, these judges should base their parole decisions on factual information, not on trivial extraneous influences. If the facts of my case merit parole, it shouldn't matter whether I come before the judge at 8 am or 2 pm. Graphing the percentage of applicants who were granted parole against the time of day, we would expect a more-or-less flat line. Yet when Danziger's team crunched ten months' worth of data, they produced the appalling graph in figure 6.5.

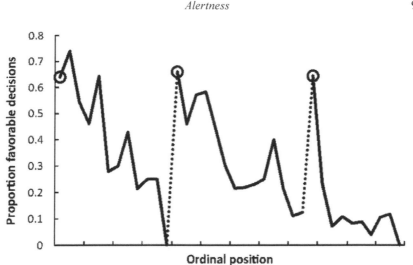

Figure 6.5   Proportion of Rulings in Favor of the Prisoners by Ordinal Position. Circled Points Indicate the First Decision in Each of the Three Decision Sessions; Tick Marks on X-Axis Denote Every Third Case; Dotted Line Denotes Food Break. *Source:* From "Extraneous Factors in Judicial Decisions," by S. Danziger, J. Levav, and L. Avnaim-Pesso, 2011, Proceedings of the National Academy of Sciences of the United States of America, Volume 108, p. 6890. Copyright 2011 by the National Academy of Sciences. Reprinted with permission.

Clearly, defendants who requested parole first thing in the day, or immediately after the judges' breaks, stood a fair chance of a favorable decision. But as each court session progressed, the defendants' chances fell practically to zero. Simply by looking at the graph, we can see that the legal facts of the matter meant less in these judicial decisions than the length of time the judge had been contemplating cases that day. By the end of each session, the judges had spent so much mental energy—so much alertness—that they simply accepted the motion on the table without having the mental drive to question it. And in this judicial system, the motion on the table is always to deny parole.

Recent educational reform in the United States has emphasized the importance of *time on task*. Principals measure it. Legislators demand it. Recesses vanish to promote it. But Danziger's research suggests that too much time on task may result in less, not more, focus. You can picture these judges, hearing case after case after case—a new one on average every six minutes. Little wonder that, after several hours, they simply don't have the mental energy to think their way through a fresh set of facts. They may be dedicated professionals, but they are also humans, and human brains can't remain constantly alert hours on end. They don't need more time on task. They need *time off task* (Ariga & Lleras, 2011).

This suggestion has the whiff of heresy. How can students master their standardized tests if we don't grind every minute out of their school day? And yet, given research like Danziger's, time off task seems both essential and easy to do. For a start, provide time for recess. And, even more simply, teachers can note when students' alertness levels are flagging, and pause the subject for a minute or two. Know that time off task need not be lengthy: a brief sidebar to discuss a recent school play or an athletic triumph or a political headline or a current movie—any well-timed digression may help snap students back to a helpful level of alertness.

A teacher whose graduate work focused on the Harlem Renaissance might adopt the following approach. When she feels her class beginning to sag, she might say: "By the way, your question reminds me of a funny story about Zora Neale Hurston." At this moment, every eye in the room brightens with hope. Can it be? Can they have gotten the teacher off subject? The students feign rapt attention, obviously eager to hear a funny story about anyone. They laugh at the punchline. They ask eager questions—anything to extend their mini mental vacation. The class banters a bit, perhaps a minute or two, and then returns to a discussion of subordinating quotations in an appositive. The students don't like that topic any more than they did three minutes ago, but—because they had just 180 seconds of time off task—they return to it with alertness levels restored.

Of course, you will find your own way to make this strategy work. In fact, this research may be supporting an intuition you have long followed. Some teachers tell jokes. Some comment on current events. Some ask about stories in the school newspaper. Whichever approach fits your own teaching style best, know that time off task can refresh alertness in a room that might otherwise sag into torpor.

A final comment on Danziger's research. Teachers often ask, quite plausibly, if the food that the judges ate during their breaks restored alertness levels more than the time off task. That's an excellent question, and we will turn to a discussion of food when we think about orienting in chapter 7. In Danziger's research, however, we can speculate about the effect of food, but we can't know—because the judicial records don't keep track of which judge ate what food. In other words, the presumption that food helped is a reasonable one, but Danziger's data do not allow for firm conclusions.

Movin' On (Wakin') Up

Several years ago, I attended a large teacher conference. You know the setup: smallish chairs lined up in tight rows under hotel ballroom chandeliers—perhaps one thousand earnest educators packed into a gradually warming atmosphere. Although I had slept well the night before and self-caffeinated that morning, three hours of plenary presentations lulled me into a stupor. When the third speaker approached the podium for yet another ninety-minute presentation, I foggily wondered how I would stay awake until lunch. Thankfully, the speaker wondered the same thing. He invited us all to stand in place, and led us through a rapid series of stretches. Even in my narrow space, hemmed in by chairs and paunchy teachers, I had enough room to raise my pulse and clear my thoughts. These two minutes of guided movement made the next eighty-eight minutes of learning possible.

Clearly, school policies requiring students to sit primly still can throw alertness levels off balance. Younger students, naturally bubbling with curious energy, can rapidly fill up with the need to move. Hyperalert, they have the wild-eyed energy of catnip-fueled kittens, and have just about the same chance of learning something in class. High school students, chronically sleep-deprived, struggle to fight off lethargy (Kelley, Lockley, Foster, & Kelley, 2015). Even when they want to learn, immobility drains them of energy. No matter their age, students forbidden from moving may struggle to find the moderate alertness level essential for attention.

The solution to this problem couldn't be clearer: find ways to allow, even encourage, movement. Have students write on the board; they have to move to get there. Have students break up into small groups to practice a new skill; they have to change seats to form their groups. Depending on the age of your students and the persona you bring to class, you may want to lead your students in stretches or brief theater warm-ups or funny cheers (Rodriguez & Fitzpatrick, 2014). The maneuvers that woke me up in that conference ballroom were not in any way magic; they simply perked up my alertness level, so I had the energy to take in new information. If that speaker can reenliven one thousand dazed and sore teachers with a minute or two of stretching, we can find ways to do so in our own classrooms.

Sleeping students present a particularly vexing example of the alertness problem. After all, sleeping students get little benefit from visual novelty, classroom variety, or time off task. (They are, in fact, taking time off task to an extreme.) Really, only movement can help students who are this tired. Get them on their feet, interacting with others. If this strategy doesn't work, nothing else will. In this dramatic case, the student needs some safe place to sleep, and we benefit ourselves and all our students if we help that student find one. (Chapter 7 returns to the importance of sleeping students.)

Recent research has begun to suggest that furniture might also help keep students moving. For younger students, "stand-biased" desks allow students to sit, but encourage them to stand in place. Even this slight increase in freedom can help young students burn off extra energy and remain moderately alert during class (Benden, Zhao, Jeffrey, Wendel, & Blake, 2014; Dornhecker, Blake, Benden, Zhao, & Wender, 2015). These initial research studies suggest that stand-biased desks allow an increase in activity, with modest benefits to alertness. While these effects seem to wear off after several months, we can say with some confidence that they do no harm, and might do good.

Teachers can promote our students' alertness levels with our own movements as well. Fixed and immobile behind a desk, we do little to enliven or calm our students. If, however, we strategically move throughout the room, our proximity and individual attention can moderate alertness. For example, Kelley and Gorham (1988) tested a combination of proximity and eye contact to promote alertness and learning. When researchers approached their students and made eye contact while teaching, one-third of the participants got a perfect score on a recall test. When they remained far away from their students and made no eye contact, only one-tenth did so. This simple strategy—moving around the room and making sustained eye contact with our students—can increase alertness and learning.

This general recommendation of movement does not imply an endorsement of any particular program or product. Some companies offer exercise programs with comically exaggerated research claims. For instance, a website might boast that bilateral movements reconnect both halves of the brain and thereby stimulate thought and creativity. This kind of neuro-nonsense is absurd.

Brain hemispheres are always perfectly well connected; the structure connecting them is among the largest and densest parts of the brain. Touching your right knee with your left elbow isn't making any meaningful difference in that kind of connectivity. Instead, touching your right knee with your left elbow is causing you to *move*. This movement reelevates your heart rate and clears away some mental cobwebs (Spaulding, Mostert, & Beam, 2010). We don't need fancy claims about bilateral stimulation reconnecting neural pathways. Practically any kind of movement helps because it moderates alertness levels.

So far, we have seen that psychologists and neuroscientists understand attention as a cumulative result of distinct neural subprocesses: alertness, orienting, and EA. We teachers haven't had much success telling our students to "pay attention" because those instructions require our students to do three different things—without telling them what they're not currently doing, or helping them to do it.

We will be much more effective in helping students pay attention if we first diagnose the underlying attentional problem. And if our diagnosis is that their alertness level is too low or too high, we've got several useful strategies—summarized in figure 6.6.

This guidance, of course, will prove most helpful if you apply it directly to your own teaching practice. You might take a few minutes right now to

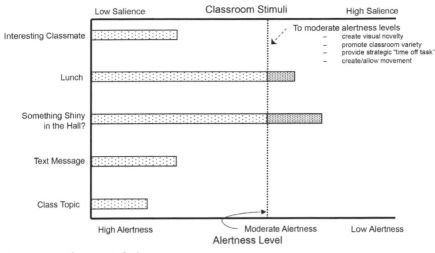

Figure 6.6 Alertness Solutions.

do so. Return to the list of attention problems you made at the beginning of chapter 5, and determine which problems on that list are alertness problems. Having made that diagnosis, consider which of these strategies you might use to solve particular problems. What posters or videos might best support the subject you teach as they also add visual novelty? How might you allow your students some cognitive downtime, and how might you bring them back to the subject? What techniques allow your students to move around the room without resulting in chaos? Every teacher will answer these questions differently, but all of the answers help moderate students' alertness levels.

Chapter Seven

Orienting

Figure 6.6 contains good news: because relatively few environmental stimuli cross the alertness threshold, the student can process those stimuli effectively. However, that diagram also shows us bad news: he is orienting to the wrong stimuli. When this student focuses on food and distractions out in the hall, he can't focus on fractions, or evolution, or St. Augustine's conversion. Once we have moderated our students' alertness levels, therefore, we must also *rebalance the salience of classroom stimuli*. We want to *decrease* the salience of stimuli that disorient the student, and *increase* the salience of the classroom topic.

In figure 7.1, the moderate alertness level ensures that the *right number* of stimuli cross the alertness threshold, while their relative salience ensures that the *right stimuli* cross that threshold.

As noted in figure 7.2, this graph organizes disorienting stimuli into two groups. The top two examples—the interesting classmate and lunch—represent *internal* distractions prompted by *biological* drives. A student disoriented by hunger or by cold is responding to basic physiology, and those bodily needs are always more salient than the subjects we teach. The third and fourth examples—the hallway trinket and the text message—represent *external* distractions: those created by *things in the environment* all around us. Chapter 7 begins by exploring strategies for reducing both internal/biological and external/environmental distractions. This mission accomplished, it then considers strategies to enhance the salience of classroom stimuli.

As you can see, we'll be covering a lot of ground in this chapter. Be sure to keep this organizational structure in mind: reduce internal distraction, reduce external distraction, and enhance classroom topic.

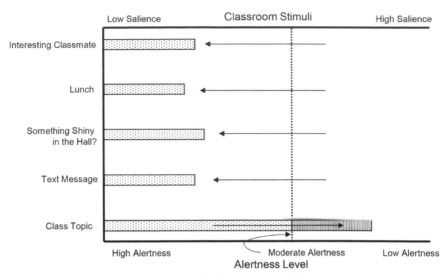

Figure 7.1 Rebalancing the Salience of Classroom Stimuli.

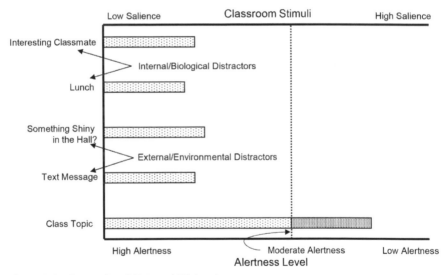

Figure 7.2 Internal and External Distractors.

ELIMINATE THE NEGATIVE, ACCENTUATE THE POSITIVE

Imagine a third scenario. You're driving to a job interview, and you are running late. The rental car company lost track of your reservation, and so you've ended up driving something from the very back of the garage. You can detect a stale whiff of cigarette smoke in the seat fabric, and the windshield wipers—did I mention that it's raining?—make the shrill scraping noise of metal etching glass. Knowing that you're behind schedule, you decided to skip lunch, but your bladder is regretting that extra coffee you guzzled down instead. The car's navigation system didn't accept the address you programmed in, and it randomly bleats out commands to turn left.

In this situation, the environment makes effective attention all but impossible. You are being drubbed by both internal/biological and external/environmental distractions. If I, sitting in the back seat, barked at you, "I can't believe you missed that turn! Why aren't you paying attention?" you would be justifiably irate. You are doing your best, but the surrounding chaos has you stumped.

In part, for example, *basic biological demands* have you thoroughly distracted. You're gut-rumblingly hungry, you really need a bathroom, and with the car's heating system stuck on high, you can hardly breathe in the tropical air. For the same reason that these biological needs have taken your focus off your urgent question—how do I get to the interview location?—they take our students' focus off essential classroom questions—what is the area under this curve? How do Buddhism and Islam describe the well-lived life? How will our group make decisions?

Ten years ago, I would have said, "these distractions are not my problems. I'm a teacher, I don't know how the heating system works in here, and if you didn't make it to the bathroom between classes then you'll just have to wait." Today I say, "anything that disorients my students is my problem, because student attention is part of my job." As a result, I have systematically rethought my responsibilities. For the same reason that I should know a lot about *Macbeth* and Nella Larsen and gerunds, I should know how human attentional systems work, and how to create an optimal classroom environment.

ELIMINATING INTERNAL/BIOLOGICAL DISTRACTORS

In order to create that optimal classroom environment, we need to start by minimizing the influence of four distractions that result from basic biological processes.

We're Having a Heat Wave

Of all the classes I have ever visited, one stands out for its quiet but memorable drama. I had been invited to see several classes that day, and so could visit this particular class for only ten minutes, but that was plenty of time to admire the remarkable classroom tone. Tenth graders had watched a video about social justice, and by the time I arrived three students had started a presentation comparing it to an earlier reading. Although the subject—race relations in the United States—can easily make students bashful or angry or hypervigilant, these presenters offered subtle, complex, and humble ideas to their peers. When I met with the teacher later that day, I complimented her on the obvious camaraderie in this class. If these students could discuss so fraught a topic with such wisdom and humility, they had connected more maturely than any I could remember.

There was only one suggestion I had to offer: fix the radiator. Despite the extraordinary honesty and depth of this student presentation, roughly half of the students had fallen into stunned, sweaty silence—all but comatose from the heat. In the 10 minutes that I visited the class, I myself wondered if I could change into something more comfortable: perhaps a bathing suit.

Joking aside, this class was a mini-tragedy. Three students took on one of the most difficult topics imaginable, and their wise bravery was simply lost. Overwhelmed by heat, their classmates could not orient to anything but their own damp misery.

No single solution to this problem stands out, but the correct approach is easy to identify: we must decide that classroom temperature is our responsibility. Once we acknowledge that responsibility, the next steps will come. Can we jimmy the windows open, move on the fly to another classroom, or plead with the maintenance staff? Can we relax the dress code enough for students to remove overheating layers, or give chilly students three minutes to get sweaters from their lockers?

The specific solution will depend on dozens of variables unique to different schools and classrooms. But the first step we all share: knowing that students will be disoriented by physical discomfort, we must first pick up the responsibility for the physical classroom. (For a discussion of working memory and classroom temperature, see Sellaro, Hommel, Manaï, & Colzato, 2015.)

Euphemism, Please

Especially for middle and high-school teachers, discussing student bathroom needs seems flatly absurd. If sixteen-year-olds can't figure out when to take care of business, they shouldn't be driving. And yet, the logic of human attentional systems can't be escaped. Because you drank all that extra coffee, you're likelier to miss the exit that gets you to your job interview; your mind is elsewhere. When students orient to their bodily needs, they do not orient to classroom work.

In fact, middle and high-school students feel this problem more acutely because they embarrass so easily. Younger students are often blissfully unembarrassed to ask about going to the bathroom. (Exhausted parents, given shrill potty alerts in public, occasionally wish their children were a bit more embarrassed to do so.) But the onset of adolescence brings with it acute sensitivity. It may simply be impossible for a student to raise her hand and ask to go to the bathroom, because doing so reveals that she actually goes to the bathroom. The shame of this revelation may linger for a lifetime—that is, until lunch.

A scientific understanding of attention leads to this straightforward conclusion: if students have to go to the bathroom, they necessarily orient to that biological need, and therefore don't orient to the class topic. To ensure that students do orient to class, therefore, we must make it as easy as possible for students to solve this problem.

In an imaginative approach, for example, one teacher uses sign language to make bathroom requests less embarrassing. He teaches his students the letter "b," and tells them to raise their hand with a "b" when they need to be excused. Without interrupting class discussion, he simply nods at the student, who can leave the room without ever having said the dreaded word or revealed any plumbing secrets. Problem solved.

Of course, strategies vary from school to school, class to class, and teacher to teacher. Your context will determine the best solution. But the first step is always the same: we must rethink our teacherly responsibilities, and acknowledge this as a problem worthy of our focus.

For the two biological needs discussed above—temperature and plumbing—solutions are relatively straightforward. For the next two, alas, solutions are thinner on the ground.

Don't Be Hangry

Think of yourself as a student on opening day. You trudge from class to class, hearing each teacher's list of policies, expectations, and habits. One teacher, however, adds a surprising rule to the list: "it is against the rules to be hungry in this class. If you are hungry here, you are breaking a rule. If you are hungry, you MUST raise your hand and tell me, and I will pass out snacks to everyone in class. But you may never be hungry—that's against the rules."

This teacher has adopted an extreme solution, but he's solving an extreme problem. Simply put, hungry students don't learn. For obvious biological reasons, humans attend to hunger before they contemplate abstract cognitive processes. If a tribe of early *Homo sapiens* had a genetic mutation that allowed them to ignore hunger, they wouldn't become our ancestors because they wouldn't survive long enough to reproduce. Evolution rewards organisms that focus zealously on the first sign of hunger, even if that focus distracts those organisms from trigonometry.

A recent meta-analysis of thirty-six studies looking at the effects of breakfast on school work, for example, found evidence that the first meal of the day benefits both memory and attention (Adolphus, Lawton, & Dye, 2013). Specifically, of nineteen studies looking at classroom behavior, more than half found that breakfast boosted on-task behavior—no matter the economic background of the students. In the cautious language of research, the authors note that this improvement "may indicate that children who eat breakfast are more able to concentrate, pay attention, and are more alert at school" (p. 23).

Unlike the biological drives discussed above, the need for food creates difficulties that individual teachers cannot easily solve. Teachers, after all, rarely have control over the lunch schedule. But as before, the first step must be to accept that problem as our responsibility—or, at least, as the school's responsibility. Once we accept that responsibility, we will take the best action we can:

- Can we add a second snack to the day?
- Can we give students a few minutes to grab an apple from their lockers?
- Can we reschedule a test so that it doesn't fall the period before lunch, when hunger can be at its worst?
- Can we raise a ruckus at a faculty meeting to insist that the lunch period be earlier and longer?

Given the certain knowledge that hunger will disorient our students, all adults who care about schools should focus zealously on this problem.

Hormones

Few teachers want to think too much about this topic. However, once puberty kicks in, basic biological drives insist that students orient to one another. Teachers might find Boyle's law sexy, but our students don't find it nearly as sexy as that classmate right over there.

For different reasons, this problem is as hard to solve as the food problem. Nonetheless, if we put our minds to the question, we can make incremental progress. We might, as deftly as possible, arrange and assign seats to minimize disorientation. (And, when doing so, we must be sure not to blame one group for the misbehavior of another.)

Here again, however, we can't simply claim that this problem isn't our job. Anything that disorients our students impedes their learning, and student learning is our job. Even if we can't do very much to reduce this problem, we should do everything we reasonably can.

Our students' interest in one another reintroduces the sleepy student mentioned in chapter 6. As any high-school teacher knows, nothing is more compelling than the dozing student across the room. Her peers watch in morbid fascination for that gripping moment when her head actually hits the desk. No doubt they also wonder how the teacher will react. Is an eruption of teacherly fury about to energize class discussion?

In Posner's language, the sleeping student's alertness problem creates an orienting problem for all the other students. Helping this student wake up— perhaps by getting her on her feet and moving—thus solves two problems. First, she will be alert enough to learn. And second, her classmates will no longer be so badly disoriented by this drowsy drama.

To sum up, in order to reduce internal distractions, teachers should remember that basic biological drives always take mental precedence over classroom work. For the same reason that an overheated car, overfull bladder, and empty stomach disorient you as you drive to a job interview, they disorient our students as they try to master the passive periphrastic, the voyages of Magellan, or the secret to dividing fractions. The improvisational work necessary to reduce these problems might not feel like our job, but anything that distracts students from learning is indeed our job.

ELIMINATING EXTERNAL/ ENVIRONMENTAL DISTRACTORS

As you were driving to your imaginary job interview, several internal/biological distractors severely disoriented you. At the same time, several *external/ environmental distractors* also increased the difficulty of your task. The smell of the cigarette smoke, the windshield-wiper scraping, the random bleats from the navigation screen: all these distractions took your mind away from the mental work you should be doing. External distractors disoriented you in the car, and disorient our students in the classroom.

Beyond Noise Pollution

In a substantial review article, Philip Beaman (2005) summarized research on the effects of irrelevant noises. He found that, depending on several conditions, such distractions can increase errors by 30–50 percent. In one study, for example, participants copied data from note cards into a computer spreadsheet. Students who listened to irrelevant sounds, and especially those who listened to irrelevant numbers, almost doubled the number of mistakes they made while copying. As Beaman emphasized, such mistakes are "beyond the individual's control and [occur] despite the individual's best efforts" (Beaman, 2005, p. 1041). Students automatically orient to new and distracting sounds, and that disorientation makes learning more difficult.

Once again, this insight adds to our list of teacherly responsibilities. The squeaky hinges on the hallway door have nothing to do with our teaching, but they have lots to do with our students' learning. So too that lingering smell of chlorine. Teachers who spend all day down the hall from the pool grow accustomed to that curious reek, but students rarely do. We might want them just to get over it, but to quote Beaman again, their distraction is "beyond the individual's control and occurs despite the individual's best efforts" (p. 1041). Our students can orient to classwork more easily when not disoriented by strange sounds or smells.

Given our earlier emphasis on visual novelty, it's not surprising that researchers have focused on classroom decorations as well. For example, Anna Fisher's research team had kindergarten students leave class for brief science lessons in another room (Fisher, Godwin, & Seltman, 2014). For half of the students, this other room was essentially bare. For the other half, it was "furnished with potential sources of visual distraction commonly found in primary classrooms (e.g., science posters, maps, the children's own artwork)" (pp. 2–3).

Fisher videotaped the students during the class to keep track of the kindergarteners' eye movement; she also used pictures to measure their understanding of new material. In the busy room, students spent 21 percent of their time looking away from the teacher; in the sparsely decorated room, that number fell to 3 percent. Given that striking difference, little wonder that students in the decorated classroom learned only about 75 percent as much as those in the sparsely decorated classroom.

This research, however, need not prompt teachers to strip classroom walls bare. In moderation, such decorations serve an important purpose: they create a sense of belonging. As a class, we do not meet in some random, generic room. Instead, we meet in a particular space: one that belongs to us. We can highlight our belonging by appropriate decoration: some work that students have done (but, not all their work), some pictures of the teacher's Chihuahua (but, not every picture), some posters appropriate to our subject matter (please, just a few posters). We can mark this space as ours by finding a middle ground between blank walls and a riot of decoration.

In a recent review article, Peter Barrett and colleagues found that "only when a room has an intermediate level of stimulation does it have a positive effect on pupils' learning progress" (Barrett, Davies, Zhang, & Barrett, 2015, p. 129).

All this investigation into disorienting stimuli leads to a specific suggestion. At some point in the next week, look at your classroom with fresh senses. Better yet, bring along someone who hasn't been in this room before. Deliberately notice what sensory experiences stand out. Is a particular photograph dramatically brighter than all the others? Can you hear the copying machine in the next room? Has the turpentine stench overtaken the room?

These potential distractors may be easy to fix. We can take down overbright posters and finally get around to cleaning out that cabinet with all the mysterious odors. Others, however, may take more time. Lobbying your colleagues to move the copy machine to another wall just might take several faculty meetings, and a few well-timed bribery cookies. All these steps may seem far outside a teacher's job description.

Certainly, ten years ago I would have scoffed at these suggestions. And yet, given the science of attention, they now strike me as essential. Students cannot pay attention to classwork if they have been disoriented by irrelevant stimuli. To help my students learn, I must not only teach well, but also reduce those irrelevancies as much as possible. As is so often true in the world of teaching, small changes can produce impressive benefits.

This Does Not Compute

A few years ago, I spent a year in graduate school studying the intersection of psychology, neuroscience, and education. I typically sat at the back of lecture halls, and so I could see not only the professors but also the other students. Most used laptops for note taking, but truthfully they spent relatively little time taking notes. At any given moment, at least three-fourths were surfing the web: watching videos, checking Facebook, or hunting down deals on Amazon.

Remember, these were graduate students of education. They believed in school. They believed in teaching and learning. They had taken on substantial debt in order to change the world one student at a time. And most of them spent most of their classroom time one click away from kitten videos.

When we discussed the Dark Side of the Force in Part I, we looked at Faria Sana's study showing how much laptops can distract students. Internet multitasking reduced a student's meteorology quiz score by 11 percent; sitting behind a multitasking peer reduced that score by 17 percent (Sana, Weston, & Cepeda, 2013). Clearly—as 6,055 Canadian high-school students will tell you—laptops and tablets can do terrible things to focus (Karsenti & Fievez, 2013).

Other kinds of technology disorient students as well. Several researchers have studied texting during class, and their conclusions reinforce common sense (Kuznekoff, Munz, & Titsworth, 2015; Rosen, Lim, Carrier, & Cheever, 2011). The more that students text during a lecture, the less they remember. Those who read texts as soon as they arrive remember less class material than those who wait for an opportune pause.

In another study, researchers observed middle school, high school, and college students working in their typical study environments: bedroom desk, dining room table, living room floor (Rosen, Carrier, & Cheever, 2013). The researchers wanted to know how often—if at all—these students looked at Facebook or sent off a text while doing homework. The answer? Every 6 minutes. Clearly, technology has great power to distract students from their academic work.

In the midst of these gloomy statistics, we should pause to remember the extraordinary benefits that academic technology provides. As I write this chapter, I'm composing on a word processor, looking up article summaries in a database, locating articles on Google Scholar or in my cloud storage, opening them in Adobe Acrobat, and double-checking my reference formats on a college web page. Our students can use various forms of technology to quiz themselves and each other, create mind maps, storyboard videos, and talk with experts and peers across the globe. Every day, teachers use apps and gadgets and Khan Academy to guide, inspire, and instruct. Technology is not the enemy of learning.

When technology disorients our students, however, it is the enemy of *attention*. When students orient to irrelevant technological stimuli—email alerts, friendly texts, and scandalous tweets—they no longer orient to their cognitive work, and therefore learn less. In this way, Facebook resembles the sound of those leaf blowers outside your classroom window; both make one of the attentional subprocesses harder to achieve.

As has been true before in this chapter, solutions will vary depending on your classroom context, but will always begin the same way: we must accept that technological distractions are our problems. With that conviction in mind, we can think about these problems in two categories: *exotic* and *domestic*.

Exotic Technology

Like exotic species that invade a biological niche, exotic technologies have no inherent place in the classroom. Relatively few teachers, for example, ask their students to use cell phones or smart watches for class work. (If you do, then think of those devices in the *domestic* technology category below.) In these cases, we search for the most effective way to remove them completely from our students' attentional field. Some teachers have students surrender phones when they arrive in the classroom, or put them in a specially designated bin at the front of the classroom.

Some researchers suggest that "tech breaks" might make exotic technologies less salient. They reason that, if students trust they will be able to reply to text messages in twenty minutes, they won't need to steal furtive glances down at a cell phone screen right now (Rosen, Lim, Carrier, & Cheever, 2011;

Rosen, Carrier, & Cheever, 2013). Your students' age doubtless will influence this category. Few first graders have smart watches. Some eighteen-year-olds—who are, after all, old enough to serve in the military—might resent surrendering their cell phones.

The only strategy that simply won't work is the strategy I once used: assume that everything will be fine. If reading text messages is as harmful and yet as common as Rosen's research finds, my professional responsibilities require me to limit the distractions that come from exotic technologies. Research does not yet offer clear guidance on the most effective strategy. Until it does, teachers must take this experimentation on ourselves.

To paraphrase Roosevelt's famous speech at Oglethorpe University, the problem of distracting technology demands bold, persistent experimentation. It is common sense to take a method and try it: if it fails, admit it frankly and try another. But above all, try something. The students who are disoriented should not sit by distracted forever while the solutions might be discovered by imaginative and perceptive teachers.

Domestic Technology

Like domestic species in a biological niche, domestic technologies do have a natural role in the classroom. Students might use the Internet to look up Renaissance depictions of Jerusalem, or a tablet for an instructive reading game, or an e-reader to follow along in the text, or a spreadsheet to create a pivot table. In these cases, we can't simply banish laptops to book bags. We must instead try to reap the benefits of technology while avoiding the weeds.

First, especially with older students, we might share the research described above. Faria Sana's studies show that off-task Internet searches lower understanding by a full-letter grade, and that sitting behind someone doing those searches damages understanding even further. Especially if we remind students of these consequences, they may be likelier to avoid such distractions.

Teachers often face a common and galling problem with domestic technologies: bells and whistles. We encourage (or allow, or require) our students to use a particular program: for example, PowerPoint for a presentation. When they begin working with that technology, however, the students quickly become engrossed with all the fancy features—dramatic fonts, flashy transitions, and elaborate graphics. Because they orient to the fun but meaningless features, they ignore the substance of the assignment itself. We can prevent this disorientation in several ways: by emphasizing the importance of content over technological style, by friendly and persistent reminders, and by creating rubrics that explicitly reward thoughtfulness and downplay pizazz.

In brief (as summarized in figure 7.3), to reduce external distractors, we can survey our classrooms to reduce the disorienting stimuli—the sounds,

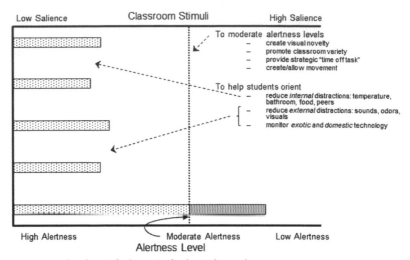

Figure 7.3   **Orienting Solutions: Reducing Distractions.**

visuals, and odors—in the environment. We can also carefully monitor our students' technology use to be sure that it enhances learning without taking focus from classroom content.

ACCENTUATING SHAKESPEARE, OR TRIGONOMETRY, OR PHONICS ...

Up to this point, we have discussed *reducing the salience of disorienting stimuli*. By accepting that the internal and external distractions in our students' lives are, in fact, our responsibility, we can work to limit their attraction: oiling squeaky hinges, making time for snacks, tucking cell phones out of sight. At the same time, we must also think about *increasing the salience of the class material we are teaching*.

Reality Check

In his books and blogs, Doug Lemov offers particularly relevant advice for boosting the salience of classroom work (Lemov, 2010, 2015). Lemov studies teaching by looking not at brains but at test scores and classrooms. In particular, he identifies teachers whose students do especially well on standardized tests, and then watches them in action. Summarizing years of inquisitive and perceptive class visitations, he describes dozens of techniques that these successful teachers use to help students learn. Although Lemov does not use the language of psychology, he does describe several techniques that help increase the salience of the class topic, and in this way promote students' attention.

One of Lemov's techniques was particularly helpful—and humbling—in my own work. For years, my students reviewed vocabulary homework during class in a predictable way. The student to my right read the first sentence out loud for the class; the next student read the next sentence; and so forth. In my thinking, this review *ought to be salient* to all my students. After all, they all need to know if they got the right answers.

And yet, as Lemov points out, this process assumes that students think about salience the same way I do. Almost certainly, they do not. Instead, the student tenth in line would quickly calculate which sentence was hers, and then look over sentence ten to be sure she felt confident about the answer. If not, she might glance at another student's vocabulary book, or even whisper a quiet question to her neighbor. Once she confirms her answer, she can think about some more interesting topic for a few minutes. Only sentence ten is salient to her, because that's the only sentence I'm requiring her to consider. I think she ought to be interested in the other answers, but she just felt a text message buzz in her pocket, and she can doubtless find out what's going on across the hall. As Lemov points out, I need a strategy that *genuinely* makes all the vocabulary sentences salient to all of the students, not one that *ought* to make them salient.

His strategy to do so requires a box and some Popsicle sticks. Each student's name goes on one Popsicle stick, and all those sticks go in the box. Now, vocabulary review has an entirely different rhythm. I announce that it's time to go over sentence one, and pause dramatically. During this pause, sentence one is salient to each student. After all, when I reach into the box and pull out one stick, it just might have their name on it. For this reason, all of my students—not just the one sitting to my right—are going over that sentence to be sure they feel confident about their answers. When I call out a name, all the other students can relax and find out if they got the right answer.

However, their respite is temporary. Now that it's time to review sentence two, again, every student knows that he or she just might be on the line as I reach dramatically for the next Popsicle stick. All of them carefully review the answer, just in case. This simple, low-tech technique makes all of the review salient for all of the students. (You may recall that, in Part I, Cuthbert's grammar teacher used this technique.)

For this technique to be fully effective, Lemov argues, teachers must pay particular attention to the Popsicle stick after we have drawn it from the box. If I set that stick aside, that student knows she is off the hook for a while. The next sentence isn't salient to her, because she knows for certain her name will not be called. To maintain high levels of salience, therefore, I should put that Popsicle stick back in the box. The student who read out sentence one just might have to read out sentence two as well—and that knowledge keeps her on her cognitive toes.

Another Lemov technique approaches the same salience problem in a different way. A lesson plan often includes a more-or-less specific list of what we will do in class today. We will, for example, start with an explanation of a particular algebraic process, and then we'll go over an example of that process, and then we'll talk about last night's homework, and then we'll go over yesterday's quiz. Equipped with such a plan, we can enter our classrooms with confidence.

With his gift for the simple-but-powerful strategy, Lemov suggests a lesson plan with two columns: the first for what the teacher is doing, the second for what the student is doing. As soon as I translate this algebra lesson plan into Lemov's two-column format, I immediately see that I am doing all the work: I'm presenting the new concept, and then I go over a few examples, and then I talk about the various problems from the homework where people struggled, and then I talk about the quiz. While I am doing all that "doing," my students are "doing" one thing: watching me while I'm doing. Once I create a dual-column lesson plans, this change in format constantly reminds me to think about the students' actual activity, and to ensure that they have specific, meaningful, and salient work to do.

From one perspective, Lemov's books offer several helpful techniques. From a different perspective, however, they offer a consistently important reminder. We should not simply focus on Popsicle sticks and two-column lesson plans; instead, we should *think about salience in a different way.* We should consider not what students *ought* to find salient, but what they *really do* find salient. As long as we are being honest with ourselves about that difference, we can employ any number of techniques to accomplish this essential goal.

This Is Only a Quiz

Teachers' efforts to make classroom work more salient can also benefit from a helpful study done by Szpunar, Khan, and Schacter (2013).

Szpunar's team invited two groups of students to watch a twenty-minute video lecture on statistics. This lecture was divided into four segments, five minutes each. Szpunar told the participants that they would have some mental work to do between each segment. For this mental work, they might randomly be assigned to solve some arithmetic problems. Or, randomly, they might be assigned to take a brief, noncumulative quiz covering the lecture segment they just watched.

Because, oddly, not everyone loves statistics, these students might have found it a challenge to focus on such a lecture. As they watched the lecture, therefore, they were occasionally asked if they were following the speaker or if they were thinking about something else. In Posner's terminology, Szpunar was checking to see if they were orienting to the lecture or not.

The researchers told participants they would be assigned to solve math problems or take quizzes randomly, but in fact there was nothing random here. Group A did math problems after the first three segments, and took a quiz only after the fourth. Group B, on the other hand, took quizzes after each segment. Groups A and B took identical quizzes after the fourth chunk of the lecture—quizzes that did not test them on material from the first three chunks.

What did Szpunar and his team learn from the data they gathered?

First, frequent quizzes increased the students' focus on the lecture. The Group A students who mostly solved math problems spent more than 40 percent of their time focusing elsewhere. In group B, the frequently quizzed students were disoriented less than 20 percent of the time. Put simply, the quizzes cut mind-wandering in half.

This result may not be terribly surprising; students who know they will be quizzed on material will orient to it more. However, we should remember that these students were participating in a psychology study. They had, literally, no incentive to do well on those quizzes—quizzes that did not cover course material, or count toward their grade, or have any effect on their lives once the study was over. These were the lowest stakes quizzes ever.

Second, Szpunar found that the students who oriented more to the lecture learned more from it. When both groups took the same quiz after the fourth segment, Group A students (who allowed their minds to wander) averaged a 70 percent. Group B students (who oriented to the lecture) averaged an 89 percent. Clearly, these quizzes both helped students orient to the lecture and improved their learning. Recall that these were not cumulative quizzes. The students in Group B did not do better because they had seen the questions before. Instead, the students in Group B did better because they had learned to orient to the lecture.

Although frequent quizzes help students orient and learn in the short run, they may very well have harmful consequences over time. Especially in this age of testing obsession, our students may very well collapse under the weight of even more assessments. Being careful researchers, Szpunar, Khan, and Schacter investigated this possibility as well. After completing the final quiz, study participants filled out a questionnaire in which they rated—among other things—their anxiety levels during the study. Drum roll please …

The Group A students, who took only one quiz, rated their anxiety levels during the study at a 4. The Group B students, who took four quizzes, rated their anxiety level at a 2.5. That's right: the students who took frequent quizzes had *lower* anxiety levels than those who took only one.

Why might frequent quizzes reduce anxiety levels? We can offer some plausible speculation. In the first place, the quizzes didn't have much weight in the students' lives. After all, even if they failed all these quizzes, those failures wouldn't really make a difference to their class grades. Again, these were the lowest of low-stakes assessments.

Second, the quizzes could very well provide pertinent feedback. As the students took the first quiz, they could see how well they had understood the content of the lecture. If they didn't know the answers on the first quiz, they could focus more intently during the following lecture segment. And if they did know the answers on the first quiz, they gained a quick shot of confidence that they were doing well already. In short, low-stakes quizzes provided helpful, even reassuring, feedback. Little wonder, then, that they might reduce anxiety.

Two final notes on Szpunar's study.

First, Szpunar and his team focused specifically on *quizzes* as a strategy to help students orient to class material. Depending on our own classroom circumstances, we might easily be able to find activities that produce the same result without looking like a quiz, or being called a quiz. Perhaps we might have teams participate in Jeopardy-like tournaments. Perhaps we have them write answers to questions on individual white boards. Perhaps we have them ask each other questions. As long as our students face regular, low-stakes challenges that prompt them to recall newly learned information, this habit will train them to orient to the material they are learning, not the sound of the cement truck in the distance.

Second, Szpunar's team studied online learning: his students watched the lecture segments and took the quizzes on a computer. This context matters, because online learners face increased difficulties with orienting. Pictures of humans are less salient than actual humans, and therefore students watching online lectures might be especially distractible. In this context, Szpunar's decision to quiz these students every five minutes makes good sense. However, when we work with real students right in front of us, our own human presence makes us more salient. In a typical classroom, in other words, a quiz every five minutes would surely be excessive.

"Tribal Classrooms"

A final key to enhance the salience of classroom work: the teacher.

With surprising frequency, research in education and psychology overlooks the teacher's role in creating learning. Because researchers so often focus on techniques—Use low-stakes quizzes! Actively monitor room temperature!—they unintentionally minimize the importance of the person using that technique. And yet, of course, teaching is not simply a collection of techniques.

In brief, students orient to classroom material because they orient to *you*; and they orient to you—first—because of your personality.

Daniel Willingham makes this point explicitly (2009). You might be a comedian, who "never misses an opportunity to use a silly example"; or a den mother, "whose students call [you] 'Mom' behind [your] back"; or a storyteller, whose class is "slow paced and low key," and who is "quiet and unassuming"; or a showman, who "puts a good deal of time and energy into thinking up interesting applications, many of them involving devices [you've] made at home" (Willingham, 2009, pp. 64–5). In each of these cases, students orient to the material not because they find it especially interesting, but because they find you especially interesting. Note the variety in Willingham's list. Many different personalities can connect students to the classroom material. But we should not overlook the fact—and we should not allow researchers to overlook the fact—that our ways of being in the world matter for learning.

Students orient to you because of your personality, and also because of their emotional connection to you and to each other. Stories of inspirational teachers abound: Anne Sullivan, Jaime Escalante, John Keating—a.k.a. Robin Williams in *Dead Poet's Society*. In each of these cases, the teacher's emotional connection with students both inspires individuals to learn and gradually links those individuals to form a classroom community.

Louis Cozolino (2013) describes this result in an arresting phrase: "the tribal classroom." Cozolino approaches this topic with an evolutionary perspective, and argues that "the more the environment of a classroom parallels the interpersonal, emotional, and motivational components of our tribal past, the more our primitive instincts will activate the biochemistry of learning" (p. 239). Although today's schools little resemble our ancestral environment, we can create communities—"tribal communities"—that emphasize this sense of belonging.

We want our classes to have their own identities, their own markers of membership, and their own *esprit de corps*. The math class that adopts pocket protectors as self-mocking badges of nerd-dom; the swim team that dyes its hair green before the big meet; the second grade section that falls in love with *Charlotte's Web* and embraces Wilbur as their mascot: all these classes build a tribal identity that teachers can use to refocus students on classroom work (Rodriguez & Fitzpatrick, 2014).

One peculiar example stands out from my own teaching experience. Early one school year, when my sophomore English class was especially rambunctious, I cried out in exasperation: "Why are you behaving like rodents?" The group immediately latched onto my insult as an honorific, and promptly dubbed themselves The Rodents. On entering the room each day, I would inquire, "How are the Rodents today?" or, "What's new with The Rodentry?" Upon raising her hand, a student might inquire "May a Rodent ask a question now?" or comment "that Rodent's point confused me." Several weeks later, when a colleague departed on sick leave, I took over his class for the rest of the term. My first class was horrified. "*They* are not Rodents," these students insisted, "WE are Rodents! You are not allowed to call them Rodents!"

This common identification, albeit bizarre, helped me corral my students to focus on the classroom topic for the day. We were a tribe; a tribe of Rodents, but nonetheless a tribe. And as a tribe, we did our English work together.

Reasonably enough, you might strive for a tribal identity with a more uplifting (and more sanitary) connotation. But whatever team identity you develop, this camaraderie draws on the neurobiology of learning to help students orient.

Over these last three chapters, we have explored our students' attention with increasing depth and subtlety—as summarized in figure 7.4. We know that, like a house under construction, attention is made up of several highly specialized parts. In chapter 6, we learned that we can moderate alertness by using visual novelty or movement.

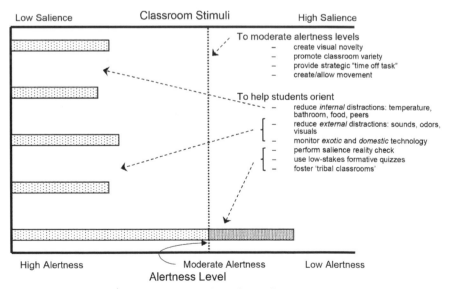

Figure 7.4   Orienting Solutions: Increasing Class Salience.

Once our students have achieved that moderate level, we need to ensure they orient to the classroom stimuli that help them learn. We can reduce the salience of disorienting stimuli in dozens of ways—primarily by accepting the responsibility for doing so. The garish posters that have been on the wall since the 1990s, the high pitched squeal coming from that florescent light bulb, that odd compost smell coming out of the sink—if they disorient our students, we must do what we can to minimize their effect on learning. Recalling Beaman's assurance that a student's distraction by these nuisances is "beyond the individual's control and [occurs] despite the individual's best efforts" (Beaman, 2005, p. 1041), we must take that job on directly and energetically.

Having reduced the salience of disorienting stimuli, we can also think about boosting the salience of our students' classroom work. Doug Lemov helps us think honestly on this topic: classroom work should be truly salient to students right now, not plausibly salient from an adult's perspective. Low-stakes formative quizzes—even if we don't call them quizzes—can also help students form the habit of orienting to their work. And Cozolino's emphasis on a "tribal classroom" reminds us of a truth we knew all along: by fostering classroom *esprit de corps*, teachers can connect students to material by the energy and zest of their personality.

Chapter Eight

Executive Attention

The last several chapters have covered a lot of ground, so before taking in new information, we should pause to review.

Here's a new review strategy: take out a blank piece of paper (or, open a new document on your computer), and write down what you have learned so far in part II. Specifically, try to answer these questions:

- How do brain researchers describe attention?
- How do they define their terms?
- What do those attention *problems* look like in classrooms?
- What kinds of *solutions* fit with each category of problem?
- What examples of those solutions did we review?
- What new ideas about your own classroom come to mind as you think back over these questions?

Give yourself several minutes to pull these pieces together.

Perhaps your review looks something like this:

Scientists do not think of attention as a single cognitive process. Instead, led by Michael Posner and others, they understand attention to be made up of distinct neural subprocesses: alertness, orienting, and executive attention.

For this reason, teachers must practice a new skill: diagnosing different root causes of attention problems.

Students routinely show too little, or too much, *alertness*, as they either doze or bulldoze their way through class. Teachers can *moderate alertness levels* by strategically using visual novelty, by wisely varying classroom activities, by giving students mental time off task, and by encouraging movement.

Students can *orient* to only a few of the thousands of the stimuli around them. As teachers, we need to reduce all the disorienting stimuli, and enhance the salience of the stimuli relevant to learning. To *reduce disorienting stimuli*, we start by rethinking our job definitions: all classroom distractions—biological, environmental, or technological—interfere with learning, and are thus our responsibility. To help students *focus on school-pertinent stimuli*, we can use Lemov's techniques and Szpunar's low-stakes quizzes to make classroom activities truly salient—not just plausibly salient—to our students. Inspired by Cozolino, we can also work to build a "tribal" spirit in our classrooms.

When you tried to summarize the third subprocess of attention, *executive attention*, you may well have been less sure what to write. The time has come to bring greater clarity to this often-puzzling topic.

By the way, if this chapter seems more difficult than earlier ones, take heart. We have saved this topic for the end because it brings together so many concepts from the entire book. This kind of summary project is helpful, but does make for cognitive challenges. As you know, new combinations of information dramatically increase WM load for our students and for teachers.

When you first considered executive attention (EA), you looked at pairs of numbers and pointed to the ones with a higher value. That simple task became surprisingly tricky when the lower numbers were printed in a larger font than the higher ones. In that case, your cognitive systems were processing conflicting information. For example, the number 3 was "smaller" than 5 in one meaning of the word, and "bigger" in another meaning, and you had to tease out which meaning to rely on. Especially under time pressure, that sorting process felt like a strange additional mental burden.

Of course, our students always have multiple cognitive possibilities to disentangle. The environment has thousands of stimuli. And, their long-term memory systems have lots of potentially relevant information tucked away. To do any kind of school work, students need to sort pertinent and meaningful information from the rest. EA allows students to focus on just a few pieces of a nearly infinite puzzle.

What, then, does an EA mistake look like? If a student's EA processes have broken down, how will we know? What is a student with such a problem *doing*?

Let's return to an example you've already pondered. In chapter 5, when you asked Jacob to identify the part of speech for the word "poodle," he called it a metaphor. Of course, "metaphor" is never the right answer to that question; after all, "metaphor" is not a part of speech but a *figure* of speech. What on earth was happening inside Jacob's head that caused him to produce this bizarre answer?

Most likely, Jacob simply had too many different kinds of information rattling around in his brain. In today's class, you discussed parts of speech.

In yesterday's class, you defined several poetry terms. In Friday's class, you went over the cast list for *Much Ado About Nothing*—defining "deputy," "Don," and "drunkard" along the way. When called upon to answer a question about poodles, Jacob recalled information from all of these lessons and—overwhelmed by possibilities—grabbed at the first answer that seemed vaguely plausible.

Jacob's struggle resembles yours when you were pointing at large numbers. One thought stream told you that 3 was larger (physically); another thought stream told you that 5 was larger (in value). In order to point correctly, you had to separate those competing thoughts. Poor Jacob, however, has so many thought streams coming at him—Synecdoche! Borachio! Conjunctive Adverb! Trochee!—that he simply can't disentangle them. The result: an almost random answer—one that looks like Jacob was *thinking about the problem the wrong way*.

Of course, Jacob probably wasn't really thinking about the problem the wrong way; he was seizing on some word that sounded familiar and hoping that he seized right. But teachers, assuming some kind of thought processes, often infer that Jacob's answer resulted from an odd mental adventure. On the outside, it looks like he's thinking the wrong way. On the inside, he's not so much thinking as scrambling.

To return to our diagnostic question: what is a student with an EA problem doing? That student is saying or doing something that causes you to think: "where did *that* answer come from? What off-topic, off-kilter cognitive process produced such a strange result?"

Here again, EA errors look different for students in each of our classes. Perhaps a student applies a phonics rule to answer a question about her favorite part of a story. Or perhaps she uses a division shortcut to solve a problem with exponents. Or perhaps she uses a velocity equation to solve a magnetism problem. Internally, the student feels muddled by too many cognitive choices. Externally, she seems to be thinking about the problem from some quirky perspective.

Although EA problems can be difficult to diagnose, happily, they are perfectly possible to solve. Once again, attention researchers have ideas that can reinforce and guide our teacherly instincts. In the rest of chapter 8, we will consider four strategies to promote EA: strategies involving fruit salad, clocks, grimaces, and laundry.

Chocolate Cake

As you thought about all the information rattling around in Jacob's head, you may well have wondered to yourself about his working memory load. If that thought occurred to you, pause to pat yourself on the back. As you have inferred, a student with an overloaded WM may well lose their ability to sort information in the way that EA requires (Fougnie, 2008).

Thus, if you spot a student struggling with an EA problem, you can use the strategies discussed in part I to reduce WM load. We can be confident in this strategy not only because it sounds so plausible, but also because it has been tested—and tested in particularly amusing way.

To determine if working memory load had an effect on executive attention, Shiv and Fedorikhin asked two groups of students to undertake a remembering-while-processing task (1999). These students had to follow directions to walk from one room to another (that's the processing) while they had to keep a specific number in mind (that's the remembering). For half of those students, the WM load was very light because they had to remember only two digits: perhaps, 26. The other half of the students carried a weighty WM load of seven digits—perhaps, 2659314.

How did Shiv and Fedorikhin measure the effect of WM load? Wickedly. They told study participants that part of their payment would be a free snack after the study was over. As they walked from the first to the second room, the students stopped at a small cart to look at their snack choices: fruit salad or … chocolate cake.

Of course, these participants knew that they ought to choose the fruit salad. And, of course, they were tempted by the cake. How successful were they at focusing on the appropriate thought process ("fruit is a healthy and nutritious part of my diet") and averting their focus from an unhelpful thought process ("mmmmmm: rich, chocolaty goodness")?

The answer depended on one more variable. Once the participants arrived at the second room, Shiv and Fedorikhin gave them a list of adjectives, such as "careless," and asked them to rate how well those words described themselves. Based on these self-ratings, the researchers could divide the participants into two further groups—those who were relatively more *impulsive* and those who were relatively more *prudent*.

Figure 8.1 combines all these data sets: WM load, snack choice, and relative prudence or impulsiveness.

The left two columns of this graph show the participants facing low-WM demands. These students had to remember only two digits—hardly a challenging task. Under these conditions, both prudent and impulsive snackers managed their cognitive processes well. When they heard a quiet internal voice saying "look at that yummy chocolate," they were able to turn away from that voice and hearken to the voice saying "fruit has few calories, and is high in dietary fiber." When WM demands were low, in other words, EA functioned well for both groups. In this way, these participants resembled you when you ignored the internal voice saying "the font of that 3 is so large" and listened to the voice saying "the value of 5 is larger than 3."

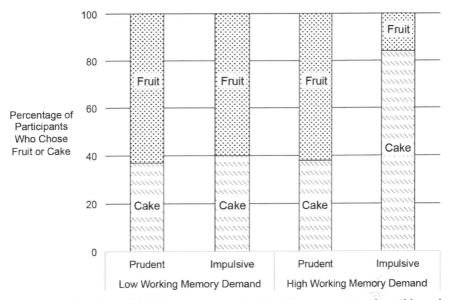

Figure 8.1   The Effect of WM Load on Executive Attention. *Source*: **Based on Shiv and Fedorikhin (1999).**

The right two columns show the participants facing high WM demands—those who had to recall seven digits. The prudent participants—that's the third column—still managed their EA processes well. Even under WM strain, they still talked themselves out of the cake and into a healthy snack. In other words: for prudent students, WM load made no difference.

In the final column ... well, the wheels came off. When *impulsive* students ran out of WM capacity, they could no longer exercise EA effectively, and chose cake more than 80 percent of the time. These students resemble you when the font size of the 3 made it so tempting that you couldn't stop yourself from pointing at it—even though you knew that 5 has a higher value.

In sum, *impulsive* students under a *high WM load* lose the ability to think correctly about a problem. WM load does influence EA success.

Even if you hadn't seen this study, you might well have thought to yourself: if a student gives me an answer that sounds like she was thinking about the problem the wrong way, I'd be tempted to reduce the WM demands. Now that you have seen the study, you can be even more confident in this impulse. When you lower WM demands, you move your students out of the right two columns and into the left two columns, and—especially for your impulsive students—that move will boost EA function.

This technique, albeit straightforward, does raise a few questions. First, how do we know which of our students are impulsive?

Answers to this sensible question boil down to this: you don't really need to worry about diagnosing that distinction. In the first place, the prudent students think about problems the wrong way less often, so you don't have to fix the mistakes they don't make. Second, teachers can readily identify impulsive students; "impulsiveness" isn't a hidden trait. Third, children—and especially adolescents—are on average more impulsive than adults. In brief, if you see an EA problem, you can try a WM solution and not really worry about impulsiveness as a variable.

Second, how much should the WM demand be reduced? As is so often true in schools, teachers must find the middle way. If the oddity of the student's answer suggests EA collapse, then I should reduce WM demands. Yet if my student answers my revised question without any thought whatsoever, I've reduced those demands too far. Like Goldilocks, I want the problem that is difficult enough (to require cognitive effort), but not too difficult (resulting in EA collapse.)

One more discussion of Jacob's poodle may help with this distinction. When Jacob says that "poodle" is a metaphor, as we've noted, his bizarre answer suggests he's thinking about the problem the wrong way.

But let's imagine a different mistake. You ask Jacob for the part of speech for "poodle" in this sentence: "We want Fluffy to visit the fancy, new poodle hotel." He contemplates this sentence for a moment and answers "noun." In this case, his answer is wrong, but not out-of-left-field wrong. After all, "poodle" almost always is a noun—you had to do some tricky thinking to create a sentence in which it is an adjective. (What kind of hotel is it? It's a *fancy* hotel. It's a *new* hotel. It's a *poodle* hotel.) In other words, Jacob got the answer wrong, but he's on the right track: he did not think about the problem in entirely the wrong way.

In this case, you probably don't need to reduce the WM level of the problem. Instead, you might ask some pertinent follow-up questions: "If 'poodle' is a noun, then it could be the subject of the sentence. Is it? Perhaps the direct object?" After just a few of these questions, Jacob will realize that "poodle" isn't a noun in this sentence. "Well, Jacob, if it isn't behaving like a noun, what part of speech is it behaving like? Is it doing what verbs do? Is it doing what pronouns do?" With these questions, you are keeping the WM load high, and helping Jacob shuffle through possible arrangements on his mental end table.

If, however, he calls poodle a metaphor, no amount of reshuffling will help. He has too many possibilities on that end table to create a coherent thought process. At this point, you need to take some information off that end table—in other words, you need to reduce the WM load.

In chapter 3, we discussed ways to think about reducing WM load. Now might be an excellent time to think through those strategies with EA in mind. Take a moment to answer these questions: can you recall a moment of EA failure—that is, when your student produced an answer than simply made no sense? What question was she trying to answer? How could you reduce the WM load of that question? More specifically, how could you reduce the WM load of that question while still giving that student enough of a cognitive challenge? Take a minute or two to write down your thoughts.

Measuring a Reservoir

In part I, we discussed the wicked imagination of psychologists. To study the effect of pressure on WM, you recall, Beilock and Carr (2005) gave students challenging math problems and then pretended to videotape them. Roy Baumeister likewise made use of psychologists' deviltry to explore an essential human characteristic: *willpower*.

In particular, Baumeister wanted to test a hypothesis that was—at the time he tested it—quite revolutionary (Baumeister & Tierney, 2011; Muraven & Baumeister, 2000). He imagined willpower as a reservoir that people draw from when we need to resist an extra desert, or decline a last glass of wine, or do the last five homework problems for a particularly boring unit. If we keep drawing on that reservoir, we might finally run out of willpower. Of course, that reservoir refills over time, but it can be temporarily drained.

In other words, willpower isn't something that you have or you don't. It is a characteristic that we have more or less of at any given moment, depending on present circumstances.

This reservoir hypothesis sounds straightforward enough, but how to test it? Did you say, radishes?

Yes, Baumeister said radishes.

His experiment was simple, and a little bit funny. When study participants came to his psychology lab, they were asked not to eat the food in the waiting room: radishes. After several minutes, they went to another room where they had to do a boring proofreading task. Specifically, they saw two columns with strings of letters and numbers, and they had to be sure that strings in both columns were identical. This dull proofreading task required willpower because few people feel intrinsic motivation to do it well.

A second group of participants were also asked not to eat the food in the waiting room, and asked to complete the same dull proofreading task. This time, however, Baumeister took away the radishes and replaced them with chocolate chip cookies. In some versions of this study, they even baked the cookies in the lab to ensure that the scent wafted through the waiting room.

Baumeister reasoned that these participants faced two willpower tasks. First, they had to resist the food in the waiting room. And second, they had to grind their way through dull proofreading. For the radish group, however, that first willpower task wasn't very hard. For most people, eating raw radishes simply isn't especially tempting. Thus, if Baumeister's hypothesis were correct, the radish group should have a lot of willpower left over for the proofreading task, and they should do quite well at it.

The cookie group, however, had a different story to tell. For most of us, resisting cookies takes quite a bit of willpower—especially because Baumeister scheduled this study right before lunch. Because these participants had to use more willpower resisting cookies than the first group used to resist radishes, they should have considerably less willpower left over to compare 495F96L with 495F69L. And for that reason, their score on the proofreading test should be relatively bad.

Sure enough, the results of this study lined up well with Baumeister's prediction. In fact, different versions of this research paradigm have been used for decades, and quite consistently support the conclusion that we can drain (and refill) our willpower reservoirs.

Teachers should notice an important point from this research paradigm: all acts of willpower drain the same reservoir. We don't have one willpower store to resist food and a second store to make ourselves do boring things. For this reason, Baumeister notes, making a list of several New Year's resolutions is a bad idea—at least if we start them all at the same time (Baumeister & Tierney, 2011). The willpower I use to cut down on desserts reduces my supply to get my essays graded more quickly, and both drain my capacity to be nicer to my in-laws. Baumeister suggests choosing one resolution, and starting work on the second only after I've made real progress on the first.

This conclusion gives teachers powerful insight into our students' lives. After all, students must constantly exert all kinds of willpower: resisting the impulse to shout out the answer, ignoring their best frenemies, and forcing themselves to get out of bed (or, at an earlier age, stay in bed). And, each of these efforts interferes with their EA, which is—after all—effortful control of cognitive processes. You might say that EA is the part of willpower that students use to get their work done. All those other demands on our students' willpower make EA that much more difficult.

When teachers first understand how willpower works, we might be inclined to despair. Given these constant demands on willpower, how can our students ever succeed? Yet we have two reasons for hope. The first is that students have been succeeding, so clearly they can manage all these drains on their self-control as well as the cognitive demands of school work.

The second reason for hope: Baumeister's wicked sense of humor. Because of his radish/cookie studies over the years, we now know effective techniques for reducing willpower demands in order to enhance EA.

Tick Tock

One of Baumeister's graduate students, Mark Muraven, has performed a series of studies that can help teachers make classroom use of these insights into willpower.

Following Baumeister's model, Muraven had students perform two self-control tasks (Muraven, Gagné, & Rosman, 2008). However, he moved away from the more impish radish/cookie paradigm. (Psychologists often confirm earlier research results by testing the same concept in many different ways.) Instead, for the first self-control task, he had students retype a paragraph they saw on a computer monitor. The computer, strangely, did not display the letters that they typed. Even with this handicap, their goal was to be as fast and accurate as possible.

Half of the participants—the group who were doing the difficult version of the task—were instructed to leave out the letter "e" and all the spaces between words. Because typing is an automatic skill for many people, this second version of the task should be much more difficult, as participants had to inhibit their instinct to type these two common symbols. (If you're not convinced that this additional instruction makes the task more difficult, try doing it yourself. Even hunt-and-peck typists find this version a challenge.)

For his second measure of self-control, Muraven had students watch numbers flash one after the other on a computer screen, with a half-second gap between them. Students had to press the space bar every time they saw the number 6 followed by the number 4. This task required extended concentration—that is, it required cognitive self-control.

So far, Muraven's study more or less replicates Baumeister's research, albeit with different self-control tasks. However, Muraven added a third variable—the variable that makes this study especially interesting to teachers: time pressure. As they were typing their initial paragraphs, half of the students in both groups saw a large timer at the top of their computer screens, reminding them literally at every second how long they were taking. Muraven wanted to know if this additional time pressure made a difference. The answer is: no, and yes.

For the students who had done the easy version of the task—that is, they didn't have to leave out any letters—the time pressure made no substantive difference. Both groups made, on average, about four mistakes during the twelve-minute concentration test.

However, for the students who did the difficult version of the task—they had to leave out the "e"s and the spaces—time pressure doubled the number of mistakes. Specifically, the students who did not face time pressure made roughly five mistakes during the concentration exercise, while those who stared at that ticking clock made more than eleven mistakes. Clearly, time pressure does terrible things to cognitive self-control, that is, it weakens EA.

Thus, Muraven's research leads to a clear strategy for supporting EA: minimize time pressure.

When striving to apply this strategy, teachers quickly discover a disturbing truth; schools are, in many ways, factories that manufacture time pressure. In higher grades, bells constantly urge both teachers and students from classroom to classroom, topic to topic. In every grade, student queries produce inevitable answers: "that's a fascinating question, but we just don't have time to answer it right now." On countless tests, the clock's second hand grimly reminds our students of the time pressure they face.

To make this first Muraven strategy work, in other words, we need to think through the specific time pressures that our own school contexts produce. Notice how often your class runs right up to—perhaps just past—the bell. Notice how often most students work on their tests up to the very last second. Notice how often you find yourself saying, "We can't take any more time with this topic; we're going to run out of time." None of these moments is—by itself—bad teaching practice. You need to worry about them only if they accompany EA failures. If you notice that students think about questions the wrong way against a background of time pressure, try to minimize that pressure as best you can.

In some cases, we can in fact make time pressure less obvious. Rather than turning a question aside because you don't have time, offer a time-neutral explanation for your decision. If your students regularly make EA-fueled mistakes at the end of tests, you can find a way to assess the material with fewer questions. Simply recognizing a habit of running class too late can trigger our determination to end with a minute to spare.

Two important points should be kept in mind. First, not all time pressure *can* be avoided. Schools are busy places. Some students process information more quickly than others. Standardized tests don't allow teachers flexibility to relieve time pressure. Don't worry about eliminating time pressure completely. Instead, focus on reducing that pressure specifically when you notice EA problems being exacerbated by it. If students are managing time pressure well—that is, if they are staring down the clock and successfully completing difficult cognitive work—that combination demonstrates real mastery of the material.

Second, not all time pressure *should* be avoided. Life includes pressure, and some of life's pressures come from time limitations. Effective adults manage these pressures well, and do so—at least in part—because they got practice as children. We should not strive to create pressure-free schools. Instead, we should find that ever-shifting balance point where pressure keeps students thinking hard without overwhelming their EA.

Motivating Environments

Muraven's first study offered teachers one specific strategy for promoting EA: reduce time pressure. In a second study, he also developed a broader series of suggestions. In it, Muraven and his colleagues drew on a well-known theory of motivation: self-determination theory (Deci & Ryan, 2000).

Since 1985, Edward Deci and Richard Ryan have argued that people are motivated by three psychological desires: relatedness, autonomy, and competence. As summarized by Muraven, they argue that "when a [student's] feelings and experiences are acknowledged, where the [student] is left free to choose a course of action that suits his or her personal needs and desires, and where the [student] is given information to make the best possible decision" (Muraven, Gagné, & Rosman, 2008, p. 2), these conditions fulfill students' basic psychological desires, and thereby enhance intrinsic motivation. Muraven's team wondered if they could support EA by deliberately promoting relatedness, autonomy, and competence.

Here again, Muraven used Baumeister's dual-task approach. For the first self-control task, participants resisted either cookies or radishes. For the second task, they performed the twelve-minute concentration exercise: pressing a space bar after seeing a 6 followed by a 4. In this study, the third variable was the behavior of the experimenter. (Apparently, part of a psychologist's wicked sense of humor includes training to be an actor.)

For one group of participants, the experimenter deliberately promoted Deci and Ryan's three motivators. To establish *relatedness*, the researcher met participants with a smile, and offered reassurance throughout her explanation of the study's procedures. To heighten a feeling of *competence*, she emphasized that this experiment—which served a valuable social function—could not happen without the participant's contribution. To highlight *autonomy*, she underlined the participant's right to choose: "We ask that you please don't eat the cookies/radishes. Is that okay?" (Muraven, Gagné, & Rosman, 2008, p. 5). In all these ways, the study design tried to promote EA by appealing to these students' psychological needs.

For the second group of participants, the experimenter reversed these behaviors. After a gruff greeting to diminish relatedness, she gave sharp instructions ("You must not eat the cookies ... let's start now") that neither acknowledged competence nor fostered autonomy. Did this difference in the experimenter's behavior change the participants' EA?

We should pause to consider the full span of Muraven's hypothesis. In this study, he first proposed that the experimenter's words and actions could change the participants' motivation. He hypothesized that a student learning from a teacher who fosters relatedness, competence, and autonomy will feel more intrinsically motivated to accomplish a particular task. He then proposed that this change in the participants' motivation could enhance their EA. Students who feel intrinsic motivation will control their cognitive processes more effectively. And within Michael Posner's theory, this increase in EA will ultimately help students pay attention. This causal chain, although plausible, might look increasingly tenuous as we contemplate all the steps that have to go according to Muraven's plan.

And yet, this causal chain worked as Muraven had predicted. When he treated students with kindness, they made on average 5.4 mistakes on the concentration task, even though their EA had been depleted by resisting cookies. When he treated them brusquely, their mistake count more than doubled, to an average of 12.3. By promoting the participants' sense of relatedness, competence, and autonomy, the experimenter dramatically reduced the number of EA mistakes they made.

This study offers teachers quite a broad range of possibilities for supporting our students' EA. Whereas Muraven's first study focuses on one specific technique—reducing time pressure—this second study allows for a long list of approaches that a teacher might use.

Fostering relatedness: we have already discussed fostering relatedness when we reviewed strategies that promote orienting. When Louis Cozolino suggests building a "tribal classroom," he emphasizes developing a sense of class identity both as a group and among individuals within that group (Cozolino, 2013). This relatedness, it turns out, not only helps students orient to you and to the material that you teach, but also helps them marshal their cognitive resources to think about that material more effectively.

Fostering competence: Deci and Ryan's strategies to foster competence emphasize the importance of positive feedback (Deci & Ryan, 2000). The more that a student knows she is doing well, the more competent she feels. This competence boosts motivation. (We saw such a process in chapter 7 when Szpunar gave students frequent quizzes during a video.) Every time a teacher catches a student doing something right, even a modest comment on that success can influence the student's sense of self.

To be clear, positive feedback can take several forms. It does not need to come directly from the teacher. In a tribal classroom, for example, students might develop the habit of congratulating one another on a newly mastered skill, a well-delivered speech, an insightfully posed question. Equally important, positive feedback does need to have a basis in reality. Compliments for shoddy work, although intended to boost students' self-esteem, do considerably more harm than good for a student's long-term cognitive and emotional development (Baumeister & Tierney, 2011).

Fostering autonomy: with your experience as a teacher, not to mention your experience as a student, you already have ideas how to promote autonomy in your classroom. The easiest strategy: whenever possible, provide appropriate choices. When students know that they have the independence to select among options, this freedom boosts their sense of autonomy. Of course, this strategy requires careful balance, for WM struggles to manage too many choices at the same time.

Deci and Ryan's research (2000) also reveals teaching habits that can imperil autonomy: an emphasis on deadlines and grades. While your class-room may reasonably require both, you can explain their importance in Deci and Ryan's terms. For example, grades help students measure the develop-ment of their own *competence*. Their intent is not to control student behavior, but to track student improvement.

Especially when contemplating autonomy, teachers might reasonably worry about implying a false promise of freedom. After all, we have a curric-ulum, and we do have to complete it. We have rules, and students must follow them. In brief, their autonomy exists within very real, and often very narrow, constraints. Yet Muraven's study gives us reason to believe that even small kinds of autonomy matter. College students who participate in these studies almost always do so to earn credit for their psychology courses. They can, in theory, refuse—as long as they are willing to write an extra paper instead. For this reason, when Muraven's experimenter asked "that you please don't eat the cookies. Is that okay?" the autonomy she implied doesn't really go very far. The participant could refuse this request, but only at the price of writing an extra essay. The researcher's words imply a freedom that barely exists.

Yet these words did create a tone, an atmosphere, a generous invitation. Rather than saying, truthfully, "you have to do this," the researcher reframed the requirement as a joint project: "would you like to be a part of this?" The underlying reality remains, but the tone implying autonomy boosted the stu-dent's motivation. So too with our own classroom work. Our students have to read the book, solve the problems, and do the lab. The words we choose and the choices we offer, however, can reframe those requirements to foster out students' sense of autonomy.

As is true for all teaching advice, these strategies will differ depending on your precise set of circumstances. Autonomy appropriate to a third grader dif-fers dramatically from that appropriate to a tenth grader. The jokey songs that might build *esprit de corps* among kindergarteners yield contemptuous eye-rolls a few years later. Your colleague might highlight competence by posting students' exemplary work, whereas you prefer complimenting them one on one. As teachers, we strive not simply to enact strict instructions offered to us by researchers, but to understand and adapt their research models to our own experience, our own schools, and our own students.

Muraven's second study, thus, suggests that we can enhance our students' EA by answering their psychological needs for relatedness, competence, and autonomy. At times, these suggestions run counter to some of our most powerful teacherly instincts. When students stop paying attention, we can switch quite quickly into the role of a disciplinarian. We insist on our power, decry their failings, and demand they do precisely what we want them to do. However, Muraven's research suggests that by reversing these priorities— by connecting rather than overpowering, by pointing out accomplishments not lapses, by allowing even modest doses of freedom rather than absolute obedience—we might enhance our students' EA and thereby keep them on task. We won't need to scold them for failing to pay attention because the atmosphere of the class has fostered their EA all along.

The precise balance for all these elements depends on many forces, including the teacher's personality. Some of us run a tight ship; some prefer a more relaxed atmosphere. As long as teachers understand the importance of EA, and recognize their own role in promoting it, many different classroom systems can work perfectly well. Muraven's studies can help us understand both why our own approaches to teaching might be working in the first place and how to enhance them if they are not.

Building a Better Model

This final section begins with a task for you to try. Ready? Simply follow these instructions ...

> The procedure is actually quite simple. First you arrange things into different groups depending on their makeup. Of course, one pile may be sufficient depending on how much there is to do. If you have to go somewhere else due to lack of facilities that is the next step, otherwise you are pretty well set. It is important not to overdo any particular endeavor. That is, it is better to do too few things at once than too many. In the short run this may not seem important, but complications from doing too many can easily arise (Bransford & Johnson, 1972, p. 722).

That's only half of the instructions, but you're probably already lost. If you're like most people, your focus began to drift after just a few sentences, and if you had to recall those instructions in a few minutes, you probably would throw up your hands and sigh. Although the sentences are grammatically correct, and the vocabulary quite simple, you just don't get enough concrete information for those instructions to make sense, or even to hold your focus.

Now, go back and reread those instructions—but this time, know that the title for that task is "doing laundry."

Once you have that new conceptual framework, those instructions make good sense. You need to sort lights from darks. If you don't have a washing machine, you need to go to the laundromat. You should beware overloading either machine. These hundred words make either no sense or perfect sense, depending on the picture you have in your head when you read them.

Researchers call the picture you have in your head a *situation model*, and such models have been studied extensively in recent decades. We can, in fact, describe learning itself as the process of updating situation models (Smallwood, Fishman, & Schooler, 2007). Students come into our classrooms with knowledge organized into particular models. They know, to take a physics example, that when they roll a marble across the floor, that marble eventually stops moving. In their situation model, like Aristotle's, objects in motion naturally come to rest.

Physics teachers provide students not only with new information, but also with new models for that information. Galileo, unlike Aristotle, understood that objects in motion remain in motion unless other forces bring them to rest. A marble rolled across a frictionless floor never comes to rest, because objects in motion remain in motion. Physics students, slowly and laboriously, learn both new information (for instance, equations describing friction) and new situation models (for instance, Galileo's conception of motion).

Most learning works this way. Students learning to read begin with the sounds they already know, and update those models by combining them with letters. Students learning fractions already have a sense that a whole is made up of parts—for instance, that a pizza has slices. They update this model with new numerical representations. History students may have heroic conceptions of founding fathers in the United States, and update those models with new information about their complexities, hypocrisies, and flaws.

When you read those laundry instructions above, you probably struggled to think about those sentences the right way; that is, you struggled with your EA. In fact, the absence of a clear situation model drastically hampered your ability to do so. Instead, your thoughts probably began to drift, your mind began to wander.

This initial wandering led to a downward cognitive spiral. Because your mind wandered, you could not use the information you read to update your situation model. Because of this even vaguer situation model, your EA had even less of a chance to kick in, and so your mind kept right on wandering. Your eyeballs might have passed over those hundred words, but your thoughts may well have been in Bora Bora.

This effect has been studied in several contexts central to education. Jonathan Smallwood, for example, has looked at mind-wandering and situation models when students read fiction (Smallwood, McSpadden, & Schooler, 2008). He asked students to read a Sherlock Holmes story, and kept track of their mind-wandering. Smallwood occasionally interrupted the students to ask if they were attending to the story or thinking of something else. He found that students whose thoughts drifted failed to update their situation models, and therefore missed key information that might help them solve Arthur Conan Doyle's mystery of *The Red Headed League*.

A second research team investigated the effect of mind-wandering on lectures (Risko, Anderson, Sarwal, Engelhardt, & Kingstone, 2012). In this study, researchers kept track of students' mind-wandering during classroom lectures. They found that, over time, students lost track of the lecture's situation model, increasingly allowed their thoughts to drift, and so missed details essential to understanding the overall argument.

These researchers hypothesize, quite plausibly, that this problem suggests its own solution (Risko, Anderson, Sarwal, Engelhardt, & Kingstone, 2012; Smallwood, McSpadden, & Schooler, 2008). If mind-wandering causes students to lose their situation model, and thus to miss essential information, teachers can reverse this process. By *routinely reestablishing the situation model*, we can limit mind-wandering, and thus help students keep track of specific information.

As an example of this hypothesis, recall your own experience. When you lacked a situation model for the first paragraph, you probably lost focus almost immediately. After rediscovering (or, in this case, discovering) the situation model in the words "doing laundry," you easily regained EA and focused on the words quite easily.

In brief, when you diagnose EA mistakes, try reestablishing the situation model.

Typical classroom practice makes this suggestion both easy and difficult to follow. Often, in a lesson plan, we start class by introducing a new concept— some new kind of situation model—and then provide students many chances to practice that particular concept. If class begins with three strategies to demonstrate that triangles are congruent, then the problems that our students solve seem to reinforce this new conceptual model. However, the practice problems that look to us like *examples of concepts* might very well feel to our students like *isolated collection of particulars*. We believe that practice strengthens situation models, and yet in real life it may instead distance our students from the very models we think they're practicing.

The solution to this quandary: frequent repetition of the situation model. In this geometry example, for instance, students should both practice the strategies and pause to discuss how they connect to the broader concepts presented at the beginning of class. If students discuss Congo Free State as an example of Imperialism, they should explicitly link Leopold II's gruesome policies to the definition of Imperialism presented the week before. Students who practice balancing chemical equations should try several examples, and should also explain how half of them exemplify the principle under discussion.

From one perspective, these suggestions seem obvious: of course we must ask our students to make such linkages. How else could they do the sophisticated cognitive work that we want them to do?

Two points, however, stand out. First, in the gritty reality of daily classroom teaching, pausing to reestablish links between example and theory can be frustratingly difficult to do. The clock is ticking, and the lesson plan says students should cover at least eight practice problems in class. If we pause to reestablish the situation model, how can we possibly cover all that ground? These studies suggest a powerful answer: if we don't pause to reestablish that model, then we might cover those examples at the price of understanding.

Second, this strategy sounds like an attempt to allow for sophisticated cognition, but it strives instead for a much more basic goal. Long before it allows for sophistication, reestablishing the situation model promotes EA. In other words, this strategy benefits not only the most advanced work that students do, but also the most introductory. In the absence of EA, our students can't really pay attention. And in the absence of attention, they struggle not only with advanced cognitive tasks, but also with the most basic work they do.

In previous chapters, you developed strategies for responding to alertness and orienting problems. In chapter 8, summarized in figure 8.2, you've studied potential responses to EA problems—that is, moments when your students seem to think about a question the wrong way. If possible, you might reduce the WM load of the problem, or minimize the time pressure they might be feeling. You could also motivate your students by promoting their relatedness, competence, and autonomy. And finally, you can reinforce the connection between examples and concepts in order to keep the situation model fresh in your students' thoughts.

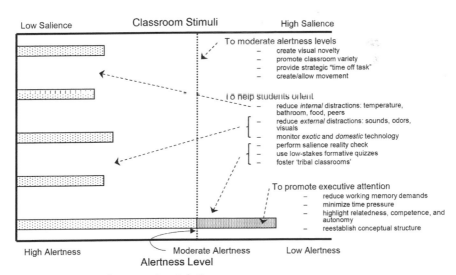

Figure 8.2   Executive Attention Solutions.

A final thought about figure 8.2. This diagram began as a simple box in chapter 5; it is now an elaborate visual structure that summarizes dozens of pages of analysis. As you consider its usefulness, ask yourself: how does this diagram help reduce WM load and promote EA?

Because you've studied part I, you know that visual representations help reduce WM load. And because you've just finished part II, you know that repetition of a situation model helps support EA. In other words, this figure both summarizes and enacts key ideas from this book.

Chapter Nine

Attention Review with FAQ

As we saw in Part I, teachers can improve our craft by understanding the central role of working memory in learning. Once we recognize the limitations we must work within, we can anticipate problems in our lesson plans, recognize them when they occur, and solve them with several research-supported strategies.

So too, a scientific understanding of attention offers teachers both a new way to think about our classroom practice and flexible strategies for acting on that new understanding.

BIT BY BIT, PUTTING IT TOGETHER

First, we now know that attention results from neural subprocesses. Just as builders create a house by constructing several specialized parts, we help our students create attention by fostering alertness, orienting, and executive attention.

Second, we know what lapses in these subprocesses look like in a classroom. Students who struggle with *alertness* are either dashing about the room (typically in younger grades) or asleep at their desks (typically in older grades). *Disoriented* students focus on stimuli in the environment other than those most pertinent to their learning. They stare out the window, or punch one another, or glance furtively at their phone screens, or sniff disdainfully at the corner cabinet where the turpentine lives. They fail to listen to the teacher or look at their books. Students low in *executive attention* don't merely get the wrong answer to questions; instead, they seem to think about those questions the wrong way. They add verbal endings to nouns, or discuss the properties of noble gasses to solve problems with metalloids, or use a subtraction shortcut to manipulate a multiplication equation.

Third, we know that we need to practice a new skill: diagnosis. In the past, we have labeled all of these problems as attention problems—and tried to solve them by crying "pay attention!" But, again, we can't create attention by focusing on attention. Instead, we must identify which of the neural processes isn't working properly; that is, we must move past a false diagnosis of an "attention problem" to the true underlying problem. Because we have spent our whole teaching careers—in fact, much of our lives—falsely diagnosing attention problem, this retraining should be a deliberate step.

As one approach to this retraining, you might visit colleagues' classrooms and observe their students. Your goal: identify behaviors that you once would have called attention problems, and label them more precisely. Distinguish the orienting problems from the EA problems, and those from the alertness problems. Once you start thinking about classroom behavior this way, most often this rediagnosis will be easy to do. However, you will be working against muscle memory, and so it will take intentional effort to hone this new diagnostic skill.

Fourth, we now have several specific strategies for supporting each of these neural functions.

To promote alertness, we can add new visual elements to the classroom: videos, for example, can help students either calm down or wake up. We can shift from one task to another: stop presenting on parallelism rules, for instance, and give students a quick chance to quiz each other on yesterday's theorem about congruent triangles. With an off-topic inquiry about yesterday's basketball game, or an editorial in the school paper, or the dance concert from last weekend, we can provide our students with brief mental breaks that will recharge their cognitive engines. And by creating movement, we can help them let off steam (in younger grades) or get their blood flowing again (in older grades). Simply by asking them to move into discussion groups that you just created, or by inviting five students to write answers on the board, or by having them stand up and shift down three seats, we can bring our students to a moderate level of alertness and thereby foster attention.

To help our students orient, we must both reduce the disorienting stimuli around them and enhance the salience of their school work. Eliminating potential sources of disorientation might seem dull and even trivial, but research shows the real advantages to this strategy. By deliberately reexamining our classrooms with fresh eyes (and ears and noses), we can perceive the potential distractors to which we have become accustomed over the months and years. The slamming lockers in the hallway, the distinct odor of burnt rubber, the brightly colored poster board of bygone projects: all these environmental stimuli, although benign to us, can sidetrack our students.

At the same time, we must also enhance the salience of our own work. By following Lemov's lead to ensure that classwork is truly salient to our students—not merely that it ought to be salient to them—we can refocus our students from the mere clutter around them to the cognitive tasks within them. By using frequent low-stakes quizzes, and even by creating "tribal" identities for our classrooms, we can help students focus on the ideas we want them to learn.

To foster EA when our students seem to think about a problem the wrong way, we can start with a WM solution and reduce the cognitive load of a particular task. If a student gets hopelessly muddled comparing four terms in economics, perhaps she will succeed at comparing three. So, too, Baumeister and Muraven's research suggests that we can help students reestablish cognitive self-control by reducing time pressure, and by fostering a supportive environment that helps them feel related, competent, and autonomous. And we can reduce mind-wandering by routinely reestablishing the situation model. This strategy ensures that new information fits clearly within a readily accessible conceptual framework.

When we organize classroom strategies in this way, we can see yet another reason that diagnosis must come first. If I think that my students are having problems "paying attention," I might remember hearing that movement can enhance attention. For this reason, I might have my students count off by five and move to newly established discussion groups.

This strategy could work very well if my students are struggling with alertness. However, if they are distracted, or if they are having trouble thinking about the question the right way, all this moving about might well disorient or muddle them still further. In other words, if I use an alertness strategy to solve an orienting or an EA problem, I may well exacerbate the very problem that I'm seeking to reduce. To be effective in promoting attention, correct diagnosis must always come first.

How, then, do all these pieces fit together in a real classroom?

As a U.S. History teacher, you might be putting together a lesson plan for your Monday sixth period class. You will be discussing Civil War battles: particularly the Seven Days campaign outside Richmond in 1862. The curriculum guide focuses on the importance of comparing three generals: Lee, Sherman, and McClellan.

As you think about helping your students pay attention during this lesson, you immediately notice that the class comes right after lunch. Everyone feels somewhat sluggish after midday meals (Monk, 2005), so you know that alertness will be a particular problem. For this reason, you decide to begin class with a quick video segment from Ken Burns's Civil War film. (Burns doesn't cover the Seven Days campaign specifically, but he vividly depicts the horror of Civil War battlefields.)

You have also got the photographs you took when you visited two battle-fields: Gaines's Mill and Malvern Hill. The landscape played a crucial part in these two battles, and the photographs make the importance of heights and rivers especially clear. You plan to have your students count off by four and break up into discussion groups to consider the role of topography in these battles. By creating two kinds of *visual novelty*, asking your students to *move* twice, and *changing* from full-class discussion to small group discussion and back, you have several strategies in place to moderate your students' alert-ness. Just in case, you have noted on your lesson plan that the girls' lacrosse team won in overtime on Saturday. If you need to give your students some *time off task*, you have got a handy topic to enliven them.

How can you help your students orient to this material? First, you have to be sure that the environmental distractions are well managed. Your classroom can get stuffy in the afternoon, so you need to remember to open the win-dows before you go to lunch; you might even borrow a fan to be sure that air circulation is good. You also commit yourself to an awkward conversation. A colleague whose office is across the hall from your classroom likes to grade essays over Beethoven. If your classroom door is open to keep air circulating, the drama of the ninth Symphony might well distract your eleventh graders from the drama of the Seven Days. You decide to ask him if he can keep his door closed … or even use earbuds.

You also plan to remind your students about the cell phone policy. You don't want to be Draco, but you do want them to learn, and we all know that text-message buzzes detract from learning. So, you will remind them to turn cell phones to airplane mode, and of the consequences if they don't.

You remind yourself to ensure that the material is really salient to them, not just hypothetically salient. For this reason, you plan a Jeopardy-like quiz at the end of the small-group discussions. In fact, you will tell them that those Jeopardy questions will cover points from both the full-class discussion and the small-group discussion. You might even interrupt class a few times to muse out loud: "Hmmm. you wonder if *that* point will be on the Jeopardy Big Board …" This strategy combines both Lemov's insight and Szpunar's quiz strategy. Thus, you are both *decreasing the salience of distracting stimuli* and *enhancing the salience of the material* under discussion.

So far you are feeling good about your plan, but you do have real concerns about your students' EA. The Seven Days campaign includes lots of factual material; after all, during those seven days, the armies fought six battles—most of which have two different names. If they think about all that factual information and compare three generals, they may have too much on their cognitive plates. For this reason, you decide to focus on only two of the bat-tles. Because you have those photos, Gaines's Mill and Malvern Hill are good choices. In this way, you are *reducing WM load* by reducing the number of names and facts that they'll be contemplating.

You are also going to narrow your focus to Lee and McClellan, and use a chart to get that comparison going. This graphic organizer will *reinforce the conceptual structure*—that is, the situation model—so that too much factual information doesn't lead to mind-wandering. For their homework, they can use this chart to consider General Sherman's performance during the Seven Days. In this way, you are still meeting the curriculum guide's goal.

Even after narrowing the focus of the lesson plan, you know that you have an ambitious agenda. For this reason, you are going to predetermine which of the Jeopardy questions you can cut if you need to save time. And you are going to put another note in the margin to remind yourself not to comment on how little time you have. Implied *time pressure*, after all, reduces cognitive self-control.

By reviewing your lesson plan with alertness, orienting, and EA in mind, you can be much more confident that your students will in fact pay attention. And you will achieve that goal without ever saying "pay attention!"

This thought process might sound daunting, but it quickly becomes second nature. Once you have had the awkward conversation with your colleague, once you have trained yourself not to talk about time pressure, once you have sufficiently reinforced the no-cell-phone rule, once you have built up a cache of helpfully lively videos, most of the work described above is either already complete or already second nature. These new habits will take some thinking, some time to explore and adopt and fine-tune. But as they become habits, you will see a change in your students' behavior and in their learning.

Of course, your own way of applying these strategies will differ considerably from this hypothetical U.S. History teacher's. If you're teaching third grade math, or seventh grade science, or fire-building for your Boy Scout troupe, you will think differently about your students, the content they must learn, the place where they learn it, and your own personality and experience. Scientific research does not produce a trail map to follow; it offers several compasses that you use to make your own way across the cognitive terrain before you.

ATTENTION FAQ

1. With all the research we have into attention, what is the ideal length for a class period? For instance, are longer classes better or worse for learning?

At present, we have no research suggesting that any one length of time is consistently better than any other. One recent meta-analysis, for example, examined fourteen different studies that compared class lengths from 55 to

90 minutes, and reached this conclusion: "[f]indings do not indicate that participating in [90 minute] block schedules would produce negative outcomes for pupils across subjects, but the findings on positive effects are not strong enough to recommend their implementation" (Dickson, Bird, Newman, & Kalra, 2010, p. 8). In other words, no one schedule was consistently better than another.

Although this meta-analysis presents its findings in rather negative language, its implication supports the central hypothesis of this book: *the key variable is not the schedule but the teacher*. Teachers who understand how attention works—that is, who know to focus on alertness, orienting, and EA—can teach quite effectively many in different class lengths. Schools that want to help students pay more attention need not revise their schedules. Instead, they should give teachers information about the science of attention.

Of course, schools have other reasons to update their daily schedules: to create more time for club meetings, to allow enough time for science labs, to build in short breaks to allow for cognitive downtime. In fact, high schools have one excellent reason to change their schedules: almost all high schools start too early. By pushing school start time back to 8:30 or 9:00 am, high schools can align their academic mission with adolescent biology (Carskadon, Wolfson, Acebo, Tzischinsky, & Seifer, 1998; Kelley, Lockley, Foster, & Kelley, 2015; Kirby, Maggi, & D'Angiulli, 2011; Wolfson & Carskadon, 1998).

2. You haven't talked about ADD or ADHD. How does this understanding of attention help us understand students with that diagnosis? Or, other kinds of atypical attention?

This book focuses on typical learners, and does not directly address the needs of atypical learners. In particular, students with ADD or ADHD deserve specialized counsel that falls outside the scope of this book.

At the same time, the model of attention outlined above can be helpful in understanding a crucial difference between students who do and do not have ADD. Students with these diagnoses typically (although not always) need a *higher level of stimulation* to be able to focus comfortably. When we charted the relationship between alertness and orienting in chapter 5, we said that a student's alertness level should allow only a few environmental stimuli to be consciously processed. However, students with a diagnosis of ADHD *need* that extra level of stimulation. The alertness level that benefits their learning is shifted to the left: somewhere between those shown in figures 6.2 and 6.4.

For these students, we must find strategies that allow extra levels of stimulation that don't overstimulate other students. One fifth grade teacher, for instance, described a simple strategy: she placed a strip of Velcro on the underside of a student's desk. By touching the Velcro, this student got the extra level of tactile stimulation he needed without distracting his classmates.

However, teachers reading this book should not break out the Velcro tape whenever they discover a student with this diagnosis. Again, ADD is a complex phenomenon, and any intervention should be discussed with professionals in the field.

Similarly, be aware that individual students are individuals—not agglomerations of averages. For example, most students who are looking out a window aren't paying attention to the teacher. However, some people need to break eye contact in order to concentrate on a verbal stream of information. For them, looking out the window is a sign that they are orienting to your voice. In other words, scientific information about averages can be very helpful, but we must always be open to atypical needs and behaviors.

3. You're describing these three subprocesses as completely distinct systems. Can a class, or a student, have more than one attention problem at a time?

Absolutely.

Teachers, of course, need to recognize the complex interactions among all these attentional systems—interactions that researchers haven't yet fully explored. In any one class, you are likely to see an orienting problem for this student and an alertness problem for that group over there. Your first set of solutions may, in turn, lead to an EA problem, which then requires a solution of its own.

While it may seem daunting to keep track of all those processes, remember: you've been managing attention with some degree of success already. This new framework will help you improve your classroom techniques, and will—over time—become second nature.

4. Is inattention always a bad thing? Don't students benefit from time to let their thoughts wander?

Several researchers have explored the advantages of mind-wandering (Immordino-Yang, Christodoulou, & Singh, 2012). If you had a sudden insight while taking your shower this morning—Eureka!—you aren't the first person to have done so. When students contemplate complex answers to large questions, we certainly want them to have time to muse, imagine, and drift.

However, if we want our students to learn this very topic that we're teaching right now, inattention is very bad indeed. A student won't learn from your description of quadratic equations if she is thinking about her ropes-course adventure this weekend.

As one extreme example, think of the prisoners whose parole decisions were being made by exhausted judges. The judges' low-alertness levels led to inattention, and that inattention led to injustice. Judicial mind-wandering might be helpful while contemplating the great legal questions, but it does terrible harm during the course of a parole hearing.

5. Can attention be trained? That is, can teachers improve a student's ability to pay attention the same way we can improve a student's ability to multiply fractions?

No, and yes.

Alertness and *orienting* are basic biological processes, and they don't easily respond to training. For example, our preference for visual novelty is strongly a part of our evolutionary heritage, and so it's unlikely that it can be trained away. So too, students automatically orient to loud noises, shiny objects, angry faces, and boisterous laughs. In extreme cases, we can train away these responses. For example, soldiers are trained not to be disoriented by environmental distractions that would rapidly befuddle most people. However, except in highly specialized kinds of education, we don't want to devote the time necessary to this kind of sensory retraining.

EA, however, can indeed be trained. As we grow up, almost all of us get better at exerting all kinds of self-control—including cognitive self-control. Adults are typically better at delayed self-gratification than children are, although there is always a range in both adults and children. In fact, self-control can be fostered by the requirements typical to any school. Every time that a student waits his turn, or works on problems that she isn't intrinsically motivated to do, or raises a hand instead of shouting out an answer, that student has practiced a little bit of self-control that will eventually help build up a greater reservoir. Many activities for younger children—Simon Says, Mother May I—make the development of self-control into a game.

As is always true, teachers strive for balance in helping students learn self-control. Baumeister's research has shown that people use up self-control over time, and so too many EA demands might temporarily deplete our students' supply. At the same time, we must give students some self-control work to do. First, they need the practice to improve self-control skills. Second, no social organization can function well if its members don't regulate their own behavior. Striving to keep this balance in mind, teachers will use our judgment, experience, and humility when adding to or subtracting from our students' current EA load.

Noting the importance of self-control, one group of researchers has developed a specific program for kindergarteners. Adele Diamond's *Tools of the Mind* curriculum has shown real promise in promoting several executive functions, including EA (Baumeister & Tierney, 2011; Diamond, Barnett, Thomas, & Munro, 2007). KIPP Academy explicitly emphasizes development of self-control as a goal of their schools. In their book *Willpower*, Baumeister and Tierney offer several other suggestions that have not yet been formalized into a specific self-control curriculum (Baumeister & Tierney, 2011). If your interest goes beyond *managing* your students' EA—as described above—to *enhancing* their baseline capacity, their book gives you an excellent starting place to investigate possible strategies.

6. Parts I and II talk a little bit about emotion and affect, but less than I had imagined. Isn't there important research on this topic?

Yes! In fact, emotion, motivation, and affect are so important that the entire second book in this series focuses on them.

As noted in the Introduction, we use multiple brain systems simultaneously while we learn. Working memory *and* attention *and* motivation *and* emotion *and* long-term memory systems interact with and conflict with and influence each other at our every waking moment. In this series of books, we are separating out those different mental systems for the sake of organization and clarity. But these distinctions are always artificial.

As teachers become more familiar with brain research, we will be able to consider any given lesson plan or assessment or student conversation from each of these perspectives. For the time being, we can improve our craft by understanding the science of working memory and attention.

7. Do you have any final thoughts?

If you're reading this book, you're on a great teaching adventure. You may have started that adventure at a conference or a workshop, or with the opening pages of *Learning Begins*. In any case, you're well along your way.

Like any adventure, this one will include unnerving moments. The research that made sense to you when you read it might seem hard to remember and harder to apply. A new technique may go comically off the rails. Indiana Jones might rescue you at the very edge of the precipice.

In these moments, don't lose heart. Instead, keep the goal in mind. And the goal is this: *we want our students to learn*. The more that teachers know about brains, and the more we know how that knowledge translates to practical classroom strategies, the more we can help them do so. That, after all, is the ultimate definition of teaching.

References

Adolphus, K., Lawton, C. L., & Dye, L. (2013). The effects of breakfast on behavior and academic performance in children and adolescents. *Frontiers in Human Neuroscience, 7*, 1–28.

Alfieri, L., Brooks, P. J., Aldrich, N. J., & Tenenbaum, H. R. (2011). Does discovery-based instruction enhance learning? *Journal of Educational Psychology, 103*(1), 1–18.

Alloway, T. P. (2006). How does working memory work in the classroom? *Educational Research and Reviews, 1*(4), 134.

Alloway, T. P., & Alloway, R. (2015). *Understanding working memory*. Los Angeles: Sage.

Ariga, A., & Lleras, A. (2011). Brief and rare mental "breaks" keep you focused: Deactivation and reactivation of task goals preempt vigilance decrements. *Cognition, 118*(3), 439–443.

Autin, F., & Croizet, J. C. (2012). Improving working memory efficiency by reframing metacognitive interpretation of task difficulty. *Journal of Experimental Psychology. General, 141*(4), 610.

Baddeley, A. (2003). Working memory: Looking back and looking forward. *Nature Reviews Neuroscience, 4*(10), 829–839.

Barrett, P., Davies, F., Zhang, Y., & Barrett, L. (2015). The impact of classroom design on pupils' learning: Final results of a holistic, multi-level analysis. *Building and Environment, 89*, 118–133.

Baumeister, R. F., & Tierney, J. (2011). *Willpower: Rediscovering the greatest human strength*. New York: Penguin.

Beaman, C. P. (2005). Auditory distraction from low-intensity noise: A review of the consequences for learning and workplace environments. *Applied Cognitive Psychology, 19*(8), 1041–1064.

Beilock, S. (2015). *How the body knows its mind: The surprising power of the physical environment to influence how you think and feel*. New York: Atria.

Beilock, S. L., & Carr, T. H. (2005). When high-powered people fail: Working memory and "choking under pressure" in math. *Psychological Science, 16*(2), 101–105.

Benden, M. E., Zhao, H., Jeffrey, C. E., Wendel, M. L., & Blake, J. J. (2014). The evaluation of the impact of a stand-biased desk on energy expenditure and physical activity for elementary school students. *International Journal of Environmental Research and Public Health, 11*(9), 9361–9375.

Bor, D., Cumming, N., Scott, C. E., & Owen, A. M. (2004). Prefrontal cortical involvement in verbal encoding strategies. *European Journal of Neuroscience, 19*(12), 3365–3370.

Bor, D., Duncan, J., Wiseman, R. J., & Owen, A. M. (2003). Encoding strategies dissociate prefrontal activity from working memory demand. *Neuron, 37*(2), 361–367.

Bransford, J. D., & Johnson, M. K. (1972). Contextual prerequisites for understanding: Some investigations of comprehension and recall. *Journal of Verbal Learning and Verbal Behavior, 11*(6), 717–726.

Bunce, D. M., Flens, E. A., & Neiles, K. Y. (2010). How long can students pay attention in class? A study of student attention decline using clickers. *Journal of Chemical Education, 87*(12), 1438–1443.

Carskadon, M. A., Wolfson, A. R., Acebo, C., Tzischinsky, O., & Seifer, R. (1998). Adolescent sleep patterns, circadian timing, and sleepiness at a transition to early school days. *Sleep, 21*(8), 871–881.

Carson, S. (2011, May). The unleashed mind: Why creative people are eccentric. *Scientific American Mind, 22*, 22–29.

Chase, W. G., & Simon, H. A. (1973). Perception in chess. *Cognitive Psychology, 4*(1), 55–81.

Corkin, Suzanne. (2013). *Permanent present tense: The unforgettable life of amnesiac patient, H.M.* New York: Basic Books.

Cowan, N. (2008).What are the differences between long-term, short-term, and working memory? *Progress in Brain Research, 169*, 323–338.

Cozolino, Louis. (2006). *The neuroscience of human relationships: Attachment and the developing social brain.* New York: W. W. Norton & Company.

Cozolino, Louis. (2013). *The social neuroscience of education: Optimizing attachment and learning in the classroom.* New York: W. W. Norton & Company.

Danziger, S., Levav, J., & Avnaim-Pesso, L. (2011). Extraneous factors in judicial decisions. *Proceedings of the National Academy of Sciences, 108*(17), 6889–6892.

Deci, E. L., & Ryan, R. M. (2000). The "what" and "why" of goal pursuits: Human needs and the self-determination of behavior. *Psychological Inquiry, 11*(4), 227–268.

Dekker, S., Lee, N. C., Howard-Jones, P., & Jolles, J. (2012). Neuromyths in education: Prevalence and predictors of misconceptions among teachers. *Frontiers in Psychology, 3*, 1–8. doi: 10.3389/fpsyg.2012.00429

Diamond, A., Barnett, W. S., Thomas, J., & Munro, S. (2007). Preschool program improves cognitive control. *Science, 318*(5855), 1387–1388.

Dickson, K., Bird, K., Newman, M., & Kalra, N. (2010). *What is the effect of block scheduling on academic achievement? A systematic review* (EPPI-Centre Report 1802T). Retrieved from EPPI-Centre website: http://eppi.ioe.ac.uk/cms/Default.aspx?tabid=2476

Dornhecker, M., Blake, J. J., Benden, M., Zhao, H., & Wendel, M. (2015). The effect of stand-biased desks on academic engagement: An exploratory study. *International Journal of Health Promotion and Education, 53*(5), 271–280.

Dunning, D. L., Holmes, J., & Gathercole, S. E. (2013). Does working memory training lead to generalized improvements in children with low working memory? A randomized controlled trial. *Developmental Science, 16*(6), 915–925.

Fisher, A. V., Godwin, K. E., & Seltman, H. (2014). Visual environment, attention allocation, and learning in young children: When too much of a good thing may be bad. *Psychological Science, 25*(7), 1362–1370.

Fougnie, D. (2008). The relationship between attention and working memory. In N. Johansen (Ed.), *New research on short-term memory* (pp. 1–45). New York, Nova Science Pub Inc.

Gathercole, S. E., & Alloway, T. P. (2008). *Working memory & learning: A practical guide for teachers.* London: Sage.

Gathercole, S. E., Durling, E., Evans, M., Jeffcock, S., & Stone, S. (2008). Working memory abilities and children's performance in laboratory analogues of classroom activities. *Applied Cognitive Psychology, 22*(8), 1019–1037.

Gathercole, S. E., Pickering, S. J., Ambridge, B., & Wearing, H. (2004). The structure of working memory from 4 to 15 years of age. *Developmental Psychology, 40*(2), 177–190.

Goldin-Meadow, S., & Beilock, S. L. (2010). Action's influence on thought: The case of gesture. *Perspectives on Psychological Science, 5*(6), 664–674.

Henik, A., & Tzelgov, J. (1982). Is three greater than five: The relation between physical and semantic size in comparison tasks. *Memory & Cognition, 10*(4), 389–395.

Hogan, T., Rabinowitz, M., & Craven III, J. A. (2003). Representation in teaching: Inferences from research of expert and novice teachers. *Educational Psychologist, 38*(4), 235–247.

Immordino-Yang, M. H., Christodoulou, J.A., & Singh, V. (2012). "Rest is not idleness": Implications of the brain's default mode for human development and education. In M. H. Immordino-Yang (Ed.), *Emotions, Learning, and the Brain: Exploring the Educational Implications of Affective Neuroscience* (pp. 43-68). New York, NY: W. W. Norton & Company.

Jaeggi, S. M., Buschkuehl, M., Jonides, J., & Perrig, W. J. (2008). Improving fluid intelligence with training on working memory. *Proceedings of the National Academy of Sciences, 105*(19), 6829–6833.

Kandel, E. R. (2006). *In search of memory: The emergence of a new science of the mind.* New York: W. W. Norton & Company, Inc.

Karsenti, T., & Fievez, A. (2013). *The iPad in education: uses, benefits, and challenges: A survey of, 6057 students and 302 teachers in Quebec, Canada.* Retrieved from T. Karsenti website: http://karsenti.ca/ipad/pdf/iPad_report_Karsenti-Fievez_EN.pdf.

Kelley, D. H., & Gorham, J. (1988). Effects of immediacy on recall of information. *Communication Education, 37*(3), 198–207.

Kelley, P., Lockley, S. W., Foster, R. G., & Kelley, J. (2015). Synchronizing education to adolescent biology: 'Let teens sleep, start school later.' *Learning, Media and Technology, 40*(2), 210–226.

Kellogg, R. T. (2001). Competition for working memory among writing processes. *The American Journal of Psychology, 114*(2), 175.

Kirby, M., Maggi, S., & D'Angiulli, A. (2011). School start times and the sleep–wake cycle of adolescents: A review and critical evaluation of available evidence. *Educational Researcher*, *40*(2), 56–61.

Kiyonaga, A., & Egner, T. (2013). Working memory as internal attention: Toward an integrative account of internal and external selection processes. *Psychonomic Bulletin & Review*, *20*(2), 228–242.

Klingberg, T. (2009). *The overflowing brain: Information overload and the limits of working memory.* Oxford: Oxford University Press.

Kuznekoff, J. H., Munz, S., & Titsworth, S. (2015). Mobile phones in the classroom: Examining the effects of texting, twitter, and message content on student learning. *Communication Education*, *64*(3), 344–365.

Lemov, D. (2010). *Teach like a champion: 49 techniques that put students on the path to college.* San Francisco: Jossey-Bass.

Lemov, D. (2015). *Teach like a champion 2.0: 62 techniques that put students on the path to college.* San Francisco: Jossey-Bass.

Lewis-Peacock, J. A., & Norman, K. A. (2014). Competition between items in working memory leads to forgetting. *Nature Communications*, *5*, 1–10.

Mayer, R. E. (2004). Should there be a three-strikes rule against pure discovery learning? *American Psychologist*, *59*(1), 14–19.

Mayer, R. E., Bove, W., Bryman, A., Mars, R., & Tapangco, L. (1996). When less is more: Meaningful learning from visual and verbal summaries of science textbook lessons. *Journal of Educational Psychology*, *88*(1), 64.

Medina, J. (2008). *Brain rules: 12 principles for surviving and thriving at work, home, and school.* Seattle: Pear Press.

Melby-Lervåg, M., & Hulme, C. (2013). Is working memory training effective? A meta-analytic review. *Developmental Psychology*, *49*(2), 270–292.

Miller, G. A. (1956). The magical number seven, plus or minus two: Some limits on our capacity for processing information. *Psychological Review*, *63*(2), 81–97.

Milner, B., Squire, L. R., & Kandel, E. R. (1998). Cognitive neuroscience and the study of memory. *Neuron*, *20*(3), 445–468.

Monk, T. H. (2005). The post-lunch dip in performance. *Clinics in Sports Medicine*, *24*(2), e15–e23.

Mousavi, S. Y., Low, R., & Sweller, J. (1995). Reducing cognitive load by mixing auditory and visual presentation modes. *Journal of Educational Psychology*, *87*(2), 319.

Muraven, M., & Baumeister, R. F. (2000). Self-regulation and depletion of limited resources: Does self-control resemble a muscle? *Psychological Bulletin*, *126*(2), 247.

Muraven, M., Gagné, M., & Rosman, H. (2008). Helpful self-control: Autonomy support, vitality, and depletion. *Journal of Experimental Social Psychology*, *44*(3), 573–585.

Olive, T., Kellogg, R. T., & Piolat, A. (2008). Verbal, visual, and spatial working memory demands during text composition. *Applied Psycholinguistics*, *29*(04), 669–687.

Pashler, H., McDaniel, M., Rohrer, D., & Bjork, R. (2008). Learning styles concepts and evidence. *Psychological Science in the Public Interest*, *9*(3), 105–119.

Posner, M. I., & Rothbart, M. K. (2006). *Educating the human brain.* Washington, D.C.: American Psychological Association.

Raz, A., & Buhle, J. (2006). Typologies of attentional networks. *Nature Reviews Neuroscience, 7*(5), 367–379.

Ridley, M. (1993). *The Red Queen: Sex and the evolution of human nature.* London: Viking.

Risko, E. F., Anderson, N., Sarwal, A., Engelhardt, M., & Kingstone, A. (2012). Everyday attention: Variation in mind wandering and memory in a lecture. *Applied Cognitive Psychology, 26*(2), 234–242.

Rodriguez, V., & Fitzpatrick, M. (2014). *The teaching brain: An evolutionary trait at the heart of education.* New York: The New Press.

Rose, T. (2016). *The end of average: How we succeed in a world that values sameness.* New York: HarperCollins Publishers.

Rosen, L. D., Lim, A. F., Carrier, L. M., & Cheever, N. A. (2011). An empirical examination of the educational impact of text message-induced task switching in the classroom: Educational implications and strategies to enhance learning. *Psicología Educativa, 17*(2), 163–177.

Rosen, L. D., Carrier, L. M., & Cheever, N. A. (2013). Facebook and texting made me do it: Media-induced task-switching while studying. *Computers in Human Behavior, 29*(3), 948–958.

Sana, F., Weston, T., & Cepeda, N. J. (2013). Laptop multitasking hinders classroom learning for both users and nearby peers. *Computers & Education, 62,* 24–31.

Sellaro, R., Hommel, B., Manaï, M., & Colzato, L. S. (2015). Preferred, but not objective temperature predicts working memory depletion. *Psychological Research, 79*(2), 282–288.

Shiv, B., & Fedorikhin, A. (1999). Heart and mind in conflict: The interplay of affect and cognition in consumer decision making. *Journal of Consumer Research, 26*(3), 278–292.

Simons, D. J., & Levin, D. T. (1998). Failure to detect changes to people during a real-world interaction. *Psychonomic Bulletin & Review, 5*(4), 644–649.

Smallwood, J., Fishman, D. J., & Schooler, J. W. (2007). Counting the cost of an absent mind: Mind wandering as an underrecognized influence on educational performance. *Psychonomic Bulletin & Review, 14*(2), 230–236.

Smallwood, J., McSpadden, M., & Schooler, J. W. (2008). When attention matters: The curious incident of the wandering mind. *Memory & Cognition, 36*(6), 1144–1150.

Smith, R. E. (2003). The cost of remembering to remember in event-based prospective memory: Investigating the capacity demands of delayed intention performance. *Journal of Experimental Psychology: Learning, Memory, and Cognition, 29*(3), 347–361.

Spaulding, L. S., Mostert, M. P., & Beam, A. P. (2010). Is Brain Gym® an effective educational intervention? *Exceptionality, 18*(1), 18–30.

Squire, L. R. (2004). Memory systems of the brain: A brief history and current perspective. *Neurobiology of Learning and Memory, 82*(3), 171–177.

Steele, C.M. (2011). *Whistling Vivaldi: How stereotypes affect us and what we can do.* New York: W. W. Norton & Company.

Szpunar, K. K., Khan, N. Y., & Schacter, D. L. (2013). Interpolated memory tests reduce mind wandering and improve learning of online lectures. *Proceedings of the National Academy of Sciences, 110* (16), 6313–6317.

Vogel, E. K., Woodman, G. F., & Luck, S. J. (2001). Storage of features, conjunctions, and objects in visual working memory. *Journal of Experimental Psychology: Human Perception and Performance, 27*(1), 92–114.

Walton, G. M., & Cohen, G. L. (2011). A brief social-belonging intervention improves academic and health outcomes of minority students. *Science, 331*(6023), 1447–1451.

Willingham, D. (2009). *Why don't students like school? A cognitive scientist answers questions about how the mind works and what it means for the classroom.* San Francisco: Jossey-Bass.

Wilson, K., & Korn, J. H. (2007). Attention during lectures: Beyond ten minutes. *Teaching of Psychology, 34*(2), 85–89.

Wolfson, A. R., & Carskadon, M. A. (1998). Sleep schedules and daytime functioning in adolescents. *Child Development, 69*(4), 875–887.

Index

About the Author

Andrew Watson began teaching high-school in 1988, and has been in or near classrooms ever since.

After earning a master's degree in Mind Brain Education at Harvard's Graduate School of Education, Andrew began working as a professional development consultant. Since 2012, he has worked with thousands of teachers, students, and parents in dozens of K–12 schools—from Johannesburg to Oakland, from New Hampshire to Texas. He also presents regularly at national conferences, including Learning and the Brain, and TABS-NAIS Global.

In his 16 years as an English teacher, Andrew worked at Concord Academy, Phillips Exeter Summer School, and Loomis Chaffee—where he also served as Dean of Faculty. He holds an AB from Harvard College, and an MA in English Literature from Boston University.

Andrew lived in Prague after the Velvet Revolution, working at the Charter 77 Foundation and managing a Beatles tribute band. He currently lives in Somerville, MA.

Made in the USA
Middletown, DE
05 June 2018